Baseball in the '30s

Lou Gehrig.

Baseball in the '30s

A Decade of Survival

An Illustrated History

Donald Honig

Crown Publishers, Inc.
New York

Published by Crown Publishers, Inc., 225 Park Avenue South, New York, New York 10003

CROWN is a trademark of Crown Publishers, Inc.

Manufactured in the United States of America

Library of Congress Cataloging-in-Publication Data

Honig, Donald.
Baseball in the '30s / by Donald Honig.
Includes index.
1. Baseball—United States—History I. Title. II. Title:
Baseball in the thirties.
GV863.A1H6515 1989
796.357'0973—dc19   89-616   CIP

ISBN 0-517-57250-8

10 9 8 7 6 5 4 3 2 1

First Edition

Design: Robert Aulicino

For Cathy

By Donald Honig

Nonfiction

Baseball When the Grass Was Real
Baseball Between the Lines
The Man in the Dugout
The October Heroes
The Image of Their Greatness (with Lawrence Ritter)
The 100 Greatest Baseball Players of All Time (with Lawrence Ritter; Revised Edition)
The Brooklyn Dodgers: An Illustrated Tribute
The New York Yankees: An Illustrated History (Revised Edition)
Baseball's 10 Greatest Teams
The Los Angeles Dodgers: The First Quarter Century
The National League: An Illustrated History (Revised Edition)
The American League: An Illustrated History (Revised Edition)
The Boston Red Sox: An Illustrated Tribute
Baseball America
The New York Mets: The First Quarter Century (Revised Edition)
The World Series: An Illustrated History
Baseball in the '50s
The All-Star Game: An Illustrated History
Mays, Mantle, Snider: A Celebration
The Greatest First Basemen of All Time
The Greatest Pitchers of All Time
A Donald Honig Reader
Baseball in the '30s

Fiction

Sidewalk Caesar
Walk Like a Man
The Americans
Divide the Night
No Song to Sing
Judgment Night
The Love Thief
The Severith Style
Illusions
I Should Have Sold Petunias
The Last Great Season
Marching Home

Contents

Acknowledgments

I am deeply indebted to a great number of people for their generous assistance in photo research and in gathering the photographs reproduced in this book. Special thanks are due Michael P. Aronstein of Photo File, and Pat Kelly, photo librarian at the Baseball Hall of Fame in Cooperstown, New York, and her hardworking colleagues.

For their good advice, wise counsel, and steady encouragement, I am grateful to these keen students of baseball history: Stanley Honig, David Markson, Lawrence Ritter, Andrew Aronstein, Douglas Mulcahy, Louis Kiefer, and Thomas Brookman.

Introduction

Few baseball decades are as embellished with notable names as are the 1930s. In addition to many of the titans of the 1920s who were still active, the 1930s saw the introduction of some of the game's most spectacular overachievers, youngsters who came to the diamond with the mists of legend already gathering around their feet.

Between the insidious depredations of economic collapse and the arrival of stunning young talent, the decade was, for baseball, one of survival. The game that had weathered a world war and internal turmoil (the Black Sox scandal of 1919) now had to outlast what gradually came to seem like an endless Depression. It wasn't easy. Nowhere was it easy in the 1930s.

In its way, baseball helped the country get through the despair and malaise. The game followed its schedule with unbroken stability, moving ahead confidently and self-reliantly, producing such buoyant folk heroes as Dizzy Dean and Pepper Martin of the St. Louis Cardinals Gashouse Gang, whose irrepressible exploits rang with a zest and spirit that helped penetrate the national gloom.

And there was Babe Ruth, by now an American symbol almost commensurate with Uncle Sam. Aging but still hitting, Ruth, in a vivid example of the game's invigorating continuity, faded just as a pair of April-fresh young future heroes named Joe DiMaggio and Bob Feller sent sportswriters into new adjectival extremes.

There was dynamite slugging from Jimmie Foxx and Hank Greenberg, and along with Dean's fast ball and engaging cornpone personality and Pepper Martin's headfirst dives was the self-effacing wizardry of Carl Hubbell and Charlie Gehringer, the tempests of Lefty Grove, and, of course, Lou Gehrig, whose consecutive-game streak ran through the decade like an iron cable of resolve.

Those years were filled with moments and achievements that have long since ripened into baseball legend: Ruth's "called shot" in the 1932 World Series, Hubbell's five consecutive strikeouts in the 1934 All-Star Game, Dean's 1937 injury and sudden downfall, Greenberg's 1938 challenge to Ruth's home run record, Gabby Hartnett's "homer in the gloamin'," Johnny Vander Meer's consecutive no-hitters, Feller's strikeout heroics, and many others. And like a promise of national resurgence itself, the decade ended with an unprecedented four Yankee world championships. There were, for the first time, night baseball and televised baseball.

There were dark hoverings over America in the 1930s and much arid ground; but its favorite game never paused or faltered, not in its growth, development, or excitement.

Baseball in the '30s

St. Louis Cardinal second baseman Frankie Frisch.

1·9·3·0

Among the leaves of baseball's historical calendar, 1930 remains unique. It was a year of Vesuvian eruptions at home plate, a year when the batter was king and the pitcher reduced almost to mere functionary. A plethora of high-caliber offensive records were set—by league, by team, and by player—that will in all likelihood remain forever secure, or at least until the game's guardians decide to add some further doses of vitality to the ball.

Major league baseball seems to have a policy of denying that its ball ever undergoes any changes, of either less buoyancy or more. The record books, however, speak for themselves, and no year more emphatically than 1930, particularly in the National League, where the summer was a symphony of line drives. It was the explosive climax to a decade of prodigious hitting that had begun with the introduction of the lively ball in 1920, abetted by the banning of the spitball and other "freak" pitches, and the more frequent introduction into the game of brand-new baseballs, which at the time were put into play without being rubbed up by the umpires, which made them just a bit more difficult to grip. In a game based on equitable balance between pitcher and batter, the landscape had been tilted, with the pitcher sliding to the foot of the slope.

The astonishing slugging of Babe Ruth delighted fans everywhere and certified the new game. "Inside baseball," as exemplified by the tactics of John McGraw and the searing talents of Ty Cobb—the steal, the hit-and-run, the sacrifice bunt, the snatching of runs one at a time—suddenly became passé. The titans of the diamond became men like Ruth and Lou Gehrig and Jimmie Foxx, men who not only

could rocket a ball over the fence but do it with plenty to spare.

The home run was new and exciting and in a way symbolic, too, as it helped define the character of a strong and self-confident nation that was in constant development and expansion. Babe Ruth was the flagship and in his wake was a procession of crown princes, not hitting as far maybe, and not as far as often surely, but collecting screaming line-drive hits with a frequency never seen before.

All through the 1920s the grounders shot through the infields and the line drives poured into the outfields and the long balls disappeared over the fences and the runners whirled around the bases and batting averages were pumped up higher and higher, until like something in long combustion the game exploded and blew its top and its sides and its entire balance in 1930—the year of the hitter.

The St. Louis Cardinals and their gaudy .314 team batting average were the National League champions in 1930. The Cards were managed by freshman skipper Gabby Street, a light-hitting catcher with the Washington Senators back in pre–World War I days, his best-known exploit being the snaring of a baseball dropped from the top of the Washington Monument.

The Cardinals were outhit by two clubs in this year of bombastic batting—the third-place Giants with a .319 average (the all-time major-league record) and the last-place Phillies at .315. Street's club, however, fielded a lineup of eight .300 hitters, topped by outfielder George Watkins' .373. George did it as a twenty-eight-year-old rookie, and it proved to be his year of wine and roses; he played in the majors another six years and hit over .300 just one more

1·9·3·0

time. Behind Watkins were second baseman Frankie Frisch (.346), outfielder Chick Hafey (.336), catcher Jimmie Wilson (.318), third baseman Sparky Adams (.314), first baseman Jim Bottomley and shortstop Charlie Gelbert (.304 each), and outfielder Taylor Douthit (.303). In addition, part-time outfielder Showboat Fisher batted .374 and backup catcher Gus Mancuso, .366.

The Cardinal pitching staff was topped by 15-game winning left-hander Bill Hallahan, known as "Wild Bill," not so much for his errant fast ball as for having posed sitting on a horse when in the minor leagues. Bill could be wild though, leading in bases-on-balls as well as strikeouts. Behind Hallahan was the veteran spitballer Burleigh Grimes, who posted a 13–6 record after being obtained in a June trade with the Boston Braves. Burleigh was one of the few legal spitballers left in baseball (when the spitter was outlawed in 1920 certain current practitioners of the lacquered delivery, Grimes among them, were given dispensation to continue throwing it). Right-handers Jesse Haines (13–8), Flint Rhem (12–8), and Sylvester Johnson (12–10) rounded out the Cardinals' starting rotation.

A late-season surge, which saw them win 39 of 49, brought the Cards from 12 games behind to a narrow two-game margin over Joe McCarthy's Cubs at the end.

In mid-September, the red-hot Cardinals were in Brooklyn for an important three-game series against the Dodgers. On the morning of the day he was scheduled to pitch, Rhem stumbled into the hotel red-eyed and hung over, with this astounding explanation: The night before, he had been kidnapped off the street, shoved into a car, and driven to somewhere in New Jersey, where he had been forced to guzzle Prohibition booze all night. The culprits, he said, were gamblers who didn't want him to pitch against the Dodgers. It was a bizarre story, particularly in the light of Flint's being an imbiber of legendary capacity. The idea of someone having to coerce him into gulping whiskey elicited winks and knowing smiles, but Flint stuck to his story and nobody ever really disproved it. Nobody ever really believed it, either.

McCarthy's second-place Cubs, who batted .309, had some genuine thunder in the outfield. Hack Wilson had a .356 batting average, hit his National League record 56 home runs, and drove in his all-time record 190 runs; Riggs Stephenson finished at .367; and Kiki Cuyler, .355. Cuyler scored 155 runs; shortstop Woody English, 152; and Wilson, 146. Overall, the Cubs scored 998 runs, six fewer than the Cardinals. The Cubs also had one of the league's two 20-game winners in Pat Malone, who was 20–9 (Pittsburgh's Ray Kremer, 20–12, was the other).

McCarthy, who later managed an array of great, world championship Yankee teams, always professed a special fondness for his Cub teams, with particular affection for Wilson and Malone, a couple of serious drinkers who were known to pack their hotel bathtubs with iced beer.

"They were good boys," Joe said years later. "Full of fun and always ready to play. And if anybody ever started anything on the field, they were the first ones out there, punching away. They knew how to punch, too."

John McGraw's Giants, finishing third, had the league's last .400 hitter in first baseman Bill Terry, who edged into this most select of baseball circles with a .401 mark. Bill and the rest of the league's timbermen were helped along by

Lou Gehrig.

1·9·3·0

the sacrifice-fly rule—in effect since 1926—that exempted a batter from a time at bat if he advanced a baserunner with a fly ball. The next season the rule was expunged from the books (it came back in its present, modified form a couple of decades later).

With the league hitting a bruising .303 and the collective earned-run average an all-time league high 4.97, Dazzy Vance's achievement deserves to be underlined. The thirty-nine-year-old Dodger ace's 2.61 ERA not only led, but it was more than a full run better than the runner-up's, New York's Carl Hubbell, who checked in at 3.76. Hubbell's teammate Bill Walker and Pat Malone were the only other pitchers to log ERAs under 4.00.

The last-place Phillies batted .315 and included a couple of .380 hitters in their lineup in Chuck Klein (.386) and Lefty O'Doul (.383), but a staff ERA of 6.70 helped bury the club. (Those withering batting averages and that wretched ERA were at least partially the product of a 280-foot right-field wall that ran straight across to right-center.)

The National League's bacchanal at home plate in 1930 produced the following: Hack Wilson's league home-run and major-league RBI records; Terry's .401 batting average and a .393 serving by Brooklyn's Babe Herman; Terry's league record 254 hits (tying him with O'Doul, who had had the same total in 1929); Boston's Wally Berger's rookie home-run mark of 38; Klein's league record 158 runs scored. In addition, there were the Giants' .319 team batting average and the Phillies' record 1,783 hits and all-time high 6.70 ERA. Twelve players collected over 200 hits and eleven who appeared in 100 or more games batted .350 or better. The Cardinals established a major-league record with 373 doubles and a National League high

with 1,004 runs. All sorts of league records were established, including slugging percentage and, for the eight-team league, highs in hits, doubles, total bases, runs batted in, runs scored, and on and on.

"It was a nightmare," said pitcher Bill Hallahan.

"It was a hell of a lot of fun," said .393 hitter Babe Herman.

While not as thunderous as the National League's, American League hitters in 1930 generated plenty of firepower of their own, compiling a .288 batting average, led by the Yankees' .309 (highest in that team's well-ornamented history). Twenty-seven-year-old Lou Gehrig, gradually replacing the aging Babe Ruth as baseball's premier siege gun, batted .379, hit 41 homers, and drove in 174 runs, 1 under the league record he set in 1927. At the age of thirty-five, Ruth turned in a year of 49 league-leading home runs, 153 RBIs, and a .359 batting average. The team also had center fielder Earle Combs at .344 and young catcher Bill Dickey at .339.

The best that this prodigious attack could earn, however, was a third-place finish behind Washington and pennant-winning Philadelphia. The difference lay in the pitching, verifying once again one of baseball's First Laws. The Yankees could offer only a couple of 15-game winners in George Pipgras (who also lost 15) and Red Ruffing, who was 15–5 after having been acquired from the Red Sox in an early-season trade for outfielder Cedric Durst and a check for $50,000. Washington had a 16-game winner in Lloyd Brown and four 15-game winners, which made for a quietly steady rotation; but Connie Mack's Athletics, who rolled in eight games ahead of the Senators (managed

Jimmie Foxx.

1·9·3·0

by Walter Johnson), had Lefty Grove at the top of their staff. Lefty, the greatest sure-thing pitcher until the arrival of Sandy Koufax in the early 1960s, turned in a torrid 28–5 record (and still hadn't reached his peak).

Grove led in wins, strikeouts (209), and ERA (2.54). Like Vance in the National League, Grove was the only American League pitcher to record an ERA under 3.00. (Cleveland's 25-game winner Wes Ferrell was next with 3.31.) Grove also led in appearances with 50, an unusual statistic for an ace pitcher, as Mack relieved with him 18 times.

"I never cared about that," Lefty said. "I'd start or relieve, whatever Connie wanted. He knew best."

Behind Grove was George Earnshaw, a big right-hander who some opponents claimed threw just as hard as Lefty. Earnshaw was 22–13, giving Connie's two aces a combined 50–18 record, and therein lay the pennant.

The Athletics batted .294, 15 points under the Yankee mark. The New Yorkers also outscored the pennant winners, 1,062 to 951, but had no Lefty Grove to make those runs stand up.

While they didn't quite have a Ruth-Gehrig combine, the A's came close enough with Jimmie Foxx and Al Simmons. Jimmie, whose breath-taking long-distance shots had earned him the accolade "the right-handed Babe Ruth," belted 37 homers, drove in 156 runs, and batted .335. (Jimmie also led in strikeouts with 66, lowest ever in the league for most strikeouts in a season. Cleveland's Eddie Morgan also fanned 66 times.) Simmons hit 36 homers, drove in a robust 165 runs, and batted .381, edging out Gehrig by two points for the title. But not even a .381 average could placate Al's loathing of opposing pitchers.

"He went to the plate with fire in his eyes," teammate Jimmy Dykes said. "He really hated pitchers. He had the same look in his eye during batting practice, for our own pitchers." Another teammate described Simmons as "a swashbuckling pirate of a man," one who was almost as rough as rookies as he was on enemy pitchers. "He told me I had to take batting practice with the pitchers when I first joined the club," young outfielder Doc Cramer recalled. "He wouldn't step out of the way until I told him he'd have to prove it to me himself. I couldn't believe I was talking that way to Al Simmons. But there was no other way. After that, we had no problems." But to the gentle Mack, who always knew where the priorities lay, Simmons was simply "a swell hitter" and let it go at that.

Catching for this powerful club (they won 102 games) was Mickey Cochrane, indisputable candidate for greatest catcher of all time. Mickey was never better than in 1930, batting .357 and driving and haranguing his teammates as the team's natural leader.

"Everybody called Cochrane 'fiery,'" the whimsical Dykes said. "That's all you heard. I asked him one day if he could breathe on bread and turn it into toast. But he was a tough competitor."

Mack's double-play combination had Joe Boley at shortstop and Max Bishop at second. Max was known as "camera eye" for his discriminating judgment of close pitches, and indeed he walked 128 times in 1930, earning every one of them, for nobody wanted to walk Max—the leadoff man—not with that powerful lineup behind him, which also included outfielders Mule Haas (.299) and Bing Miller (.303).

Walter Johnson's third-place Senators had a

Babe Ruth.

Hack Wilson.

lineup soaked with .300 hitters, including Heinie Manush (.350), Joe Cronin (.346), Sam Rice (.349), Sammy West (.328), and Joe Judge (.326).

Fourth-place Cleveland, with a .304 team average, joined the Yankees and Senators as .300-hitting teams. The Indians led the league with 358 doubles, which was the only significant offensive category the Yankees were not tops in. Spearheading the Cleveland assault was second baseman Johnny Hodapp with a .354 average and league-leading totals in hits (225) and doubles (51). Johnny was supported by outfielder Dick Porter (.350), first baseman Eddie Morgan (.349), and outfielder Earl Averill (.339). Third baseman Joe Sewell, long one of baseball's most uncanny practitioners because of his unique ability to put the bat on the ball, had 353 at bats this year and struck out just three times.

"Even when I was a kid growing up in Alabama," Joe said, "I'd throw bottle caps into the air and whack them with a broomstick handle. Never missed. I was just blessed with good eyesight and coordination."

Wes Ferrell, in his second big-league season was 25–13 for the Indians (after breaking in with a 21–10 record in his rookie year), but the Cleveland pitching thinned out after that.

Lefty Stewart was 20–12 for the sixth-place Browns and Ted Lyons put together a 22–15 season for the seventh-place White Sox. Of Lyons, who spent his entire 21-year career laboring for generally inept White Sox teams, Joe McCarthy said, "If he'd been pitching for the Yankees, he would have won 400 games." As it was, Ted won 260. Lyons was philosophical about the destiny that yoked him to losing teams for most of his long career. "According to some people," he said, "losing is the worst thing in the world. Well, it isn't. What's worse is allowing yourself to be eaten alive by it."

While the American League hitting did not match the National's record-busting assaults in 1930, the A.L. sluggers still doled out enough punishment to laden the pitching with a collective 4.65 ERA and hold it to just 41 shutouts, the all-time major league low. (The National League record for fewest shutouts in a season for an eight-team league is 48 in 1925.)

In the World Series, however, the hitting suddenly stopped. The Athletics batted just .197 in winning their second straight world championship, while the Cardinals posted a team average of .200. It was a six-game Series, with Grove and Earnshaw running true to form, each ace winning twice.

Lefty Grove.

Lefty Grove

He was born March 6, 1900, in Lonaconing, Maryland. His full name was Robert Moses Grove; some people called him "Mose," others "Lefty," and an awful lot of people called him the greatest left-hander of them all. The evidence for this substantial claim is clearly visible in Grove's record, one of the most unambiguous in all of baseball.

Grove came to the major leagues with the Philadelphia Athletics in 1925, breaking in modestly with a 10–13 record (the only time he was ever under .500), but leading the league in strikeouts, which he would do for his first seven years in the majors. In 1926 he was 13–13, but led in earned-run average, the first of nine times he was number one in this highly prestigious pitching statistic, a record made the more impressive when one realizes that no other pitcher has won more than five ERA titles.

Beginnng in 1927 with a 20–12 record, Grove had seven consecutive 20-game seasons, peaking with his 1930–31 records of 28–5 and 31–4, which remains the highest elevation of sustained success in all of baseball history. Overall, he won 20 or more eight times, pitching on until 1941, unwilling to leave until he had chalked up his 300th victory, retiring with a 300–141 lifetime ledger. Among twentieth-century pitchers, Grove's .680 winning percentage is topped only by Whitey Ford's .690.

The legend of Lefty Grove consists of two halves of equally prodigious proportions—his speeding, sometimes near-invisible fast ball and his cantakerous, sometimes volcanic temperament. By all account, Lefty Grove the man was quiet and modest—some teammates described him as "shy," a man ill at ease in the role of big-league celebrity.

"He never quite understood why people made such a fuss over him," one teammate said.

Lefty Grove the pitcher, however, was another matter. On the mound he could become transformed, metamorphosed in competition by what has been described as "a terrifying will to win." Lefty Grove in defeat, especially when that defeat was narrow, was a figure of unrepressed fury, known to smash chairs and lockers and equipment.

"By the next day it was all forgotten," Jimmy Dykes said. "He'd get it all out of his system and that was that. But while it was going on it was quite a show. Lefty was always quite a show."

After retiring as an active player, Grove never returned to baseball.

"I'd seen enough trains and hotels," he said. "And cities. I never liked cities. I just went fishing."

Grove died on May 23, 1975, at the age of seventy-five.

Jim Bottomley, one of the eight .300 hitters in the Cardinal lineup in 1930.

Chick Hafey posing with a rather snazzy-looking automobile.

Cardinal third baseman Sparky Adams, a .314 hitter in 1930.

Flint Rhem. He was 12–8 for the Cardinal pennant winners in 1930.

Dazzy Vance.

The Philadelphia Phillies' Chuck Klein: a sensational season in 1930.

Kiki Cuyler. The Cubs outfielder had 228 hits in 1930 and batted .355.

Cincinnati second baseman Hughie Critz. He was traded to the Giants early in the season.

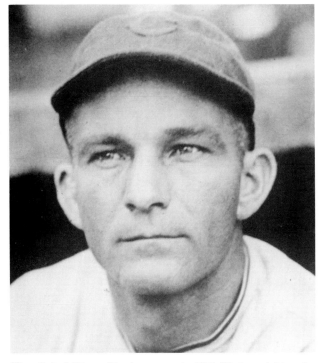

The Cubs' Riggs Stephenson. A .336 lifetime hitter, he batted .367 in 1930.

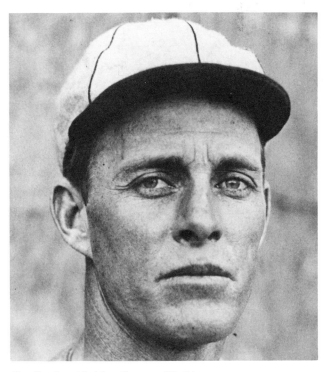

Cardinal outfielder George Watkins.

Brooklyn's Babe Herman. Along with his .393 batting average in 1930, he hit 35 home runs, had 241 hits, and drove in 130 runs.

New York Giants first baseman Bill Terry, the National League's last .400 hitter.

Pittsburgh's Pie Traynor, perennial candidate for Greatest Third Baseman of All Time. In 1930 he batted .366.

Lefty Grove.

Ray Kremer, Pittsburgh's 20-game winner in 1930. It was the veteran right-hander's last big season.

Athletics outfielder Bing Miller. In 1930 he batted .303 and drove in 100 runs.

Cochrane diving to get his man at the plate. (The base runner is unidentified.)

Al Simmons.

George Earnshaw, a 20-game winner in each of the Athletics' pennant-winning years of 1929–31.

Mule Haas, center fielder on Connie Mack's 1929–31 pennant winners.

Eddie Rommel, a veteran knuckle baller who was 9–4 for the A's in 1930.

Mickey Cochrane.

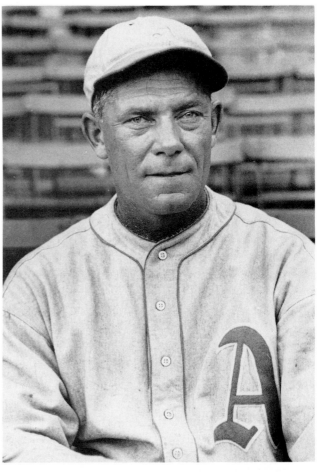

Jack Quinn. At the age of forty-six, the well-traveled right-hander was 9–7 for Connie Mack in 1930, working primarily out of the bull pen. He went to the National League the following year and pitched until 1933.

Lou Gehrig taking his cut.

The exterior of Philadelphia's Shibe Park in 1930.

Joe Judge, longtime first baseman of the Washington Senators. Joe batted .326 in 1930.

Brooklyn outfielder Johnny Frederick, who joined the batting orgy in 1930 with 206 hits and a .334 batting average.

Forty years old in 1930, Washington outfielder Sam Rice played the full season and batted .349, collecting 207 hits.

Yankee center fielder Earle Combs, a .344 hitter in 1930.

Giant third baseman Fred Lindstrom, who batted .379 in 1930, with 231 hits.

Chicago Cubs right-hander Pat Malone. He was 20–9 in 1930.

The substance of any pitcher's nightmare. *Left to right:* Jimmie Foxx, Babe Ruth, Lou Gehrig, Al Simmons.

Cleveland's 25-game-winning right-hander Wes Ferrell.

Cleveland second baseman Johnny Hodapp. In 1930 he batted .354 and led the American League with 225 hits and 51 doubles.

Joe Sewell *(left)* and brother Luke.

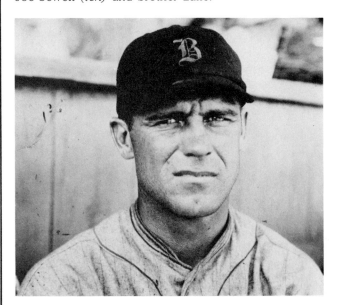

George Sisler. The great first baseman finished his career playing for the Boston Braves in 1930, batting .309.

Left-hander Walter (Lefty) Stewart, who was 20–12 for the sixth-place Browns in 1930.

Right-hander Sylvester Johnson, who was 12–10 for the pennant-winning Cardinals in 1930.

Braves outfielder Lance Richbourg.

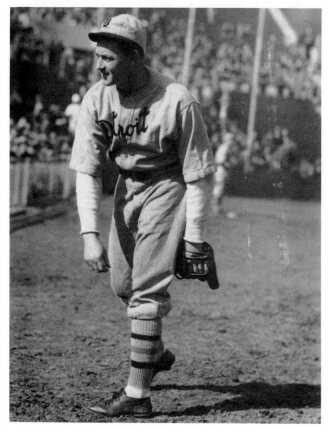

Former Yankee ace Waite Hoyt, who was traded to Detroit early in the season.

Ted Lyons, one of the Chicago White Sox' all-time great pitchers. He was 22–15 for the seventh-place Sox in 1930.

Yankee Stadium. Note how undeveloped the area around the Stadium was at the time.

George Kelly, one-time Giant first baseman, who split the 1930 season between the Reds and Cubs.

Wally Berger, whose 38 home runs set a rookie record in 1930.

Like so many others, White Sox outfielder Carl Reynolds had the year of his life in 1930, batting .359 and rapping out 202 hits.

That's Frankie Frisch nailing Mickey Cochrane on an attempted steal of second in the first game of the 1930 World Series. Shortstop Charley Gelbert is backing up. The umpire is Harry Geisel.

Willis Hudlin, a 15-game winner for the Indians in 1931.

1·9·3·1

In spite of certain farcical elements, there remains a certain compelling quality to the 1930 baseball season. The cream of the nation's favorite game had put bat to ball with a volume and resonance never seen before or since, establishing standards to whet the appetites of all who followed. Generations later, those inflated statistics read like something out of a fantasy game played before the eyes of unreliable witnesses and overly indulgent scribes. It had been an entertaining show, but the beauty of baseball lies in the sensitive balance of its structure. In 1930 the pitchers had been partially disarmed by the unnatural liveliness of the ball and the game spun crazily on an uneven axis. An entertaining spectacle, yes, but many of the game's purists were appalled, among them John McGraw, at the time one of baseball's dominant figures.

Al Lopez, then a rookie catcher for the Dodgers, recalls one incident that typified the year's cannonading and helped turn McGraw's wrath against this liveliest of lively balls.

"Roy Parmelee was pitching against us this day in the Polo Grounds, the bases were loaded, and Glenn Wright was up. Parmelee threw him a fast ball; his fast ball had a natural sliderlike break to it. Glenn started to swing, saw the pitch breaking away, and kind of half threw his bat at the ball, almost one-handed. He got out in front of it and hit it down the left-field line. Remember the Polo Grounds, how short it was down the lines? Well, Glenn hit it just hard enough for the ball to drop in for a grand-slam home run. We could see McGraw throw up his hands in the dugout, and, we heard later, he said, 'What kind of baseball is this?' I think he made up his mind right then

and there that the ball was too lively and that something had to be done. The way I understand it, that was the beginning of softening the ball up a bit."

So, like something that had undergone a winter of obedience training, the major league baseball was tamer and less spirited in 1931 than it had been in 1930.

"Naturally the owners said the ball was no different," Burleigh Grimes said. "They always said that. If that were true, then it meant that all the pitchers in baseball had improved unbelievably in one year's time."

The National League batting average dropped from .303 to .277, while the American League, with a shorter fall to make, went from .288 to .278. There were more shutouts, lower earned-run averages, fewer traumatized pitchers. A batting average—Chick Hafey's .349—considered nondescript the year before was good enough to lead the National League in 1931. (If the average was comparatively modest, then the race for the title itself was exciting: Hafey's .3489 just nosed out Bill Terry's .3486 and Jim Bottomley's .3481.)

The most precipitous personal decline was endured by the Cubs' Hack Wilson, who tobogganed from 56 home runs to 13 and from 190 runs batted in to 61, though by all accounts Hack still led the league in boozing.

Gabby Street made it two for two as a manager, his Cardinals winning their second pennant in a row, cruising in 13 games ahead of McGraw's Giants. Along with the .340 bats of Hafey and Bottomley, the Cardinals also had a .311 season from second baseman Frankie Frisch and a .300 batting average from rookie outfielder Pepper Martin, a ruggedly amiable

1·9·3·1

Oklahoman who played with a madcap fervor that was soon to characterize the team that would become known as "The Gashouse Gang."

"Pepper was our secret weapon," Bill Hallahan said years later, recalling with affection the dash and verve of the Cardinals' center fielder. "He was tough and daring and unpredictable, but never reckless; he had very good instincts on a ball field."

Hallahan with a 19–9 record was the ace of the Cardinal staff. Bill's 19 wins tied Pittsburgh's Heinie Meine and Philadelphia's Jumbo Elliott for the lead, making it the first time in its history the National League had failed to turn out a 20-game winner. Right behind Hallahan on the St. Louis staff was rookie Paul Derringer (18–8), followed by the veteran Grimes (17–9).

John McGraw was in his last full season as Giants manager. The fifty-eight-year-old New York institution was becoming increasingly surly, irascible, and, some felt, irrational. He was no longer on speaking terms with first baseman Bill Terry and barely exchanged words with outfielder Fred Lindstrom, who had this to say about his skipper: "The world had changed, the players had changed, but McGraw would have none of it; he refused to accept it." McGraw still insulted and humiliated his players with sulphurous sarcasm, as he had done decades before, when players bowed their heads and took it. But the new breed was not so docile. "It was eating him up," Lindstrom said. "You could see it: he was fighting a losing battle but remained stubbornly fixed in his ways. It was sad, and it was hell playing for him."

With a .289 team average, the Giants tied the third-place Cubs for the highest mark in the league. Terry, the greatest of all McGraw's players (and with a will and resolution to match the old man's), led a lineup that included .300 hitters Travis Jackson, Fred Leach, Lindstrom, and Shanty Hogan.

The Giants had three fine pitchers at the top of their staff in knuckle-balling Fred Fitzsimmons (18–11) and lefties Bill Walker (16–9) and Carl Hubbell (14–12). Walker (2.26) and Hubbell (2.66) were one-two in earned-run average in the league.

Running the third-place Cubs was another National League legend, Rogers Hornsby. At the age of thirty-five, Hornsby got into 100 games, batting .331 in what proved to be his last full season. Rogers was another difficult man to play for, according to young second baseman Billy Herman, who joined the Cubs late in the season, beginning what was to become a Hall of Fame career.

"Hornsby ignored me completely," Herman said, "and I figured it was because I was a rookie. But then I saw he ignored everybody. He was a very cold man. He would stare at you with the coldest eyes I ever saw. If you did something wrong, he'd jump all over you. He was a perfectionist and had a very low tolerance for mistakes."

The RBI leader was Philadelphia's Chuck Klein, who drove in 121 runs (he had had 170 the year before and finished second) and also led in home runs with 31. Klein was in the midst of a spectacular first five big-league seasons, during which he collected 200 or more hits each year, led four times in home runs, twice in RBIs, hits, and doubles, three times in slugging, and won a Triple Crown. Nevertheless, Chuck was never considered the equal of men like Bill Terry or Paul Waner because he played in Baker Bowl, where the neighborly

The Cardinals' Chick Hafey, the National League's leading batter in 1931.

Bill Hallahan, ace left-hander of the pennant-winning 1931 Cardinals. He was 19–9 and led in strikeouts.

Looking like a proud father, Connie Mack poses with Mickey Cochrane *(left)* and Lefty Grove.

1·9·3·1

right-field fence converted routine fly balls into extra-base hits. Away from home, Klein was a good hitter; in Baker Bowl he was a terror.

This was the year that the Baseball Writers Association of America began voting an award for the league's Most Valuable Player, as determined by the writers, and the National League's first MVP was the Cardinals' Frisch.

"The greatest competitor I ever saw," Bill Hallahan said of his teammate. "If he made an error in the field that cost you a run, he'd come into the dugout after the inning, his face red, snarling. 'I'll get it back for you,' he'd say, and more times than not he would, too. He'd get on first somehow—a walk, a hit, a bunt hit—and he'd steal second and then he'd come around and score, on another steal and a ground out or fly ball, some way or other. But he'd do it. That was Frisch."

The first American League player to win the MVP vote from the baseball writers was the cream of a particularly elite class—Lefty Grove of the pennant-winning Philadelphia Athletics. After turning in a near-impeccable 28–5 record in 1930, Connie Mack's moody speedballer was—hard to believe—even better in 1931, lighting up the baseball firmament with a 31–4 year.

It probably needed a 30-game season for a pitcher to win the MVP in the American League that year, for there was some truly voluminous bombardment from some familiar overachievers. Lou Gehrig hit 46 home runs, batted .341, and set an American League runs-batted-in record with 184, one of those records that doesn't need to be secured under lock and key to keep it from assault. Lou's fellow rocket launcher, Babe Ruth, checked in with a patented Babe Ruth season—.373 batting average, 163 runs batted in, and 46 home runs (tying Gehrig for

the league lead). Then there was the Athletics' Al Simmons, batting .390 and winning his second straight batting crown. Nevertheless, it was Grove's year.

With Lefty sculpting a 31–4 record, George Earnshaw 21–7, and Rube Walberg 20–12, it would have been most difficult for the Athletics not to win their third pennant in a row, and in fact they won it handily, by 13½ games over the second-place Yankees, who put on a bruising batting show all summer. In addition to Ruth and Gehrig, Joe McCarthy's club got .300+ seasons from Bill Dickey, Joe Sewell, Ben Chapman, and Earle Combs.

Once again the Yankees outhit the pennant winners (.297 to .287) and outscored them by 209 runs—1,067 to 858 (those 1,067 runs are the major-league record). But once again it was Connie Mack's superior pitching—his three aces logging a combined 72–23 record—that made the difference. McCarthy's top pitcher, Lefty Gomez, was 21–9 in his first full season.

While not as pyrotechnical as the Yankees', the Athletics' attack had plenty of sock. In addition to Simmons, Mack received a .349 year from Mickey Cochrane and .323 from Mule Haas, as well as some solid slugging from Jimmie Foxx (30 homers and 120 RBIs, which actually constituted an off-season for Jimmie). The Athletics won 107 games, earning them the distinction of being the first American League club to win over 100 games three years in a row. A 17-game winning streak (third highest in league history) in May tore the pennant race apart and it never came back together again.

But the big story of 1931 was Grove, demonstrating the awesome powers of an incomparable pitcher at his absolute peak (teaming with Cochrane to form what has to be baseball's all-time greatest battery). Nor did Lefty simply

follow his teammates' potent hitting to glory; the fireballer posted a 2.05 ERA, remarkably low for that free-swinging era (the lowest in the league, in fact, between 1919 and 1943), also leading in strikeouts (175) and tying Earnshaw for the lead in shutouts (3). And along the way Lefty turned in a 16-game winning streak that was broken by a 1–0 loss to the St. Louis Browns, the run scoring on a misplayed fly ball; after the game the tempestuous Mr. Grove nearly dismantled the clubhouse.

Despite the falloff in hitting from 1930, some notable pounding was done in the league in 1931. Ruth contributed a milestone with his 600th home run. Boston's Earl Webb, by any standards a journeyman player, established an all-time record with 67 doubles (a freakish achievement, since he never hit more than 30 in any of his six other big-league seasons). Cleveland's Wes Ferrell, a 22-game winner, set a record for pitchers with nine home runs. For Wes it was a third 20-game season in a row, all at the beginning of his career. The Cleveland ace sequined his fine year with a no-hitter against the Browns on April 29, a game in which he was fully in charge, knocking in four runs with a homer and double. The no-hitter was the first in the league in nearly five years. Another no-hitter was pitched on August 8, by Washington's Bobby Burke over the Red Sox.

Cleveland, a hard-hitting club in those years, had first baseman Eddie Morgan batting .351 and its regular outfield hoisting these figures: Earl Averill, .333 (with 143 RBIs); rookie Joe Vosmik, .320; and Dick Porter, .312. The Indians batted .296 as a unit, one point under the Yankees. But as their manager Roger Peckin-

paugh said, "With those monsters in the league"—he was referring to the A's and Yankees—"you started off the season fighting for third place." Third place this year went to Walter Johnson's Washington Senators, who won 92 games and still finished 16 behind.

Detroit's rookie right-hander Tommy Bridges won the Heartbreak Award for the game he pitched—and the game he almost pitched—against Washington on August 5. After retiring the first 26 batters he faced, Bridges was nicked for a bloop single by pinch hitter Dave Harris, depriving the Tiger right-hander of a perfect game.

The Cardinals turned loose their "secret weapon" upon the Athletics in the World Series that year—an event known in baseball lore as "The Pepper Martin World Series." Pepper stung the ball with dazzling regularity and ran the bases with splendid fervor. The Cardinals' uninhibited rookie tattooed Grove and Earnshaw and the rest of Connie Mack's staff for 12 hits and stole five bases—all in the first five games—and his exploits charmed and diverted a nation that was slipping deeper and deeper into the gloom of economic depression. The 1931 World Series, won by the Cardinals in seven games, proved once again that the October pageant provides the most accommodating stage for those who would seize baseball glory. If not for that one sizzling week in October 1931, Johnny Leonard Roosevelt (Pepper) Martin would today be a name known only to the game's more zealous archivists. But, as Frankie Frisch said years later, "Pepper got hot at just the right time and has a whole World Series named for him."

Lou Gehrig.

Lou Gehrig

Baseball hero, American legend; a player of incomparable slugging feats and unparalleled durability; a man of quiet modesty, who has probably come as close to sainthood as American sports allows, whose death was insidiously slow and agonizing. This was Lou Gehrig, "The Iron Horse," "The Pride of the Yankees," "The Crown Prince" to Babe Ruth's kingship.

The robust slugging record he compiled looks on the printed page almost as unreal as his personal story sounds. "He always showed up, he never complained, he never caused trouble, and he always hit." That was Joe McCarthy's affectionate, appreciative, and succinct summation of his favorite player, and it could well stand as Gehrig's epitaph.

The man who became the embodiment of the corporate Yankee image was born in New York City on June 19, 1903, just a few months after the Yankees entered the American League.

Conspicuous as a hard hitter in high school and then at Columbia University, which he attended on a sports scholarship, Gehrig sipped a few cups of coffee with the Yankees in 1923 and 1924 before permanently taking over first base on June 2, 1925, when the longtime regular Wally Pipp reported with what has become baseball's most celebrated headache.

Unlike Ruth, Gehrig was not a pronounced pull hitter. He hit "screamers" in all directions and, unlike most of the top home-run hitters, had more lifetime doubles than homers (535 to 493). And like his only rivals for left-handed-hitting-power supremacy, Ruth and Ted Williams, his career average is extremely high— .340. He batted over .370 three times, reaching his pinnacle with .379 in 1930.

Five times he hit over 40 homers in a season, twice reaching 49. It is as an RBI man, however, that Gehrig reigns supreme, averaging nearly one RBI (.92) per game over his career (equaled only by Hank Greenberg, who played in far fewer games). With Ruth and Foxx he holds the major-league record with 13 years of over 100 RBIs, with those 13 years being consecutive, another record he shares with Foxx.

Gehrig drove in over 150 runs in a season seven times, over 170 three times, with his 184 in 1931 the American League record. Swinging against the heady competition of Ruth, Foxx, and Greenberg, he led in home runs three times and RBIs five times, while winning a Triple Crown in 1934.

For seven World Series he batted .361, once more showing his RBI consistency with 35 in 34 games.

Gehrig died on June 2, 1941, a few weeks before his thirty-eighth birthday.

Pepper Martin.

The veteran Jesse Haines, who was 12–3 for the Cardinals in 1931.

Pepper Martin ripping one in the 1931 World Series. Mickey Cochrane is the catcher.

Al Simmons, the American League's leading hitter in 1931 with a .390 average.

Paul Derringer. The Cardinals' rookie right-hander was 18–8 in 1931.

Outfielder Taylor Douthit, who was traded from the Cardinals to the Reds early in the 1931 season.

Rube Walberg, who was 20–12 for the Athletics in 1931.

Athletics shortstop Joe Boley.

Lloyd Waner, Paul's younger brother and Pirate teammate. Lloyd batted .314 in 1931 and led the league with 214 hits.

Washington Senator pitcher Bump Hadley. He pitched for four American League teams during the 1930s.

Paul Waner, a three-time National League batting champion. In 1931 the Pirate star batted .322.

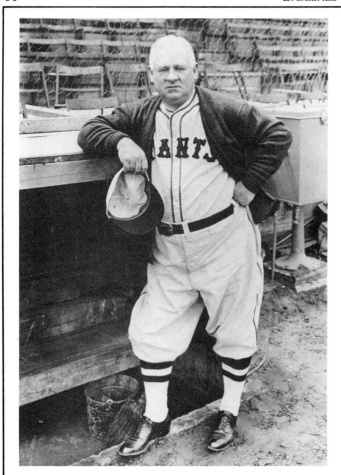

John McGraw.

Max Bishop, second baseman on the 1929–31 Athletics pennant winners. Known as "camera eye," Max drew well over 100 walks in each of those years.

Just twenty-one years old in 1931, Cleveland right-hander Mel Harder had a long and distinguished career ahead of him.

New York Giant catcher Frank (Shanty) Hogan.

Born in Cleveland, outfielder Joe Vosmik made good in the local ball yard, batting .320 in 1931, his rookie year.

In 1931, the thirty-seven-year-old veteran Burleigh Grimes had one of his best seasons, helping the Cardinals to the pennant with a 17–9 record.

George Grantham, who split his time between first base and second base for the Pirates in 1931. He batted .305, the eighth (and last) consecutive season he was over .300.

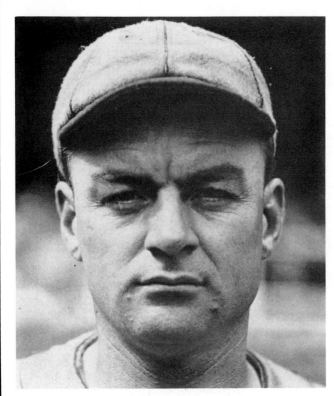

Cardinal catcher Jimmie Wilson.

Babe Ruth.

Phillies third baseman Pinky Whitney.

Larry French. Crafty rather than overpowering on the mound, the Pittsburgh left-hander was 15–13 in 1931.

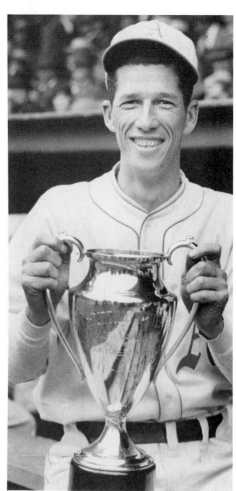

The usually dour Lefty Grove clearly is pleased with the cup he received for being the American League's Most Valuable Player in 1931.

It looks like the Babe has popped it straight up.

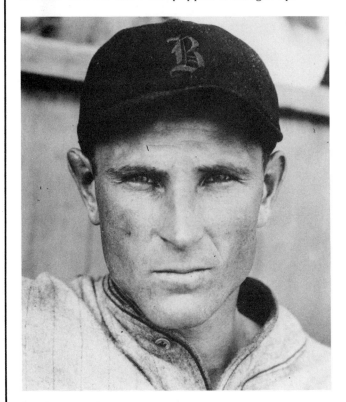

Ed Brandt. The Braves left-hander was 18–11 for a seventh-place team in 1931.

The Phillies' Spud Davis, a catcher with a .308 lifetime average. He batted .326 in 1931.

Chicago Cubs manager and second baseman Rogers Hornsby. He batted .331 in 1931, an indication that the thirty-five-year-old slugger—whose lifetime average is .358—had begun to slip.

Lou Gehrig making the putout at first. The runner is the Athletics' Eric McNair.

Athletics third baseman Jimmy Dykes. When Connie Mack finally retired in 1950, Jimmy was the man he picked to succeed him.

Jimmie Foxx has the full, rapt attention of his young fan as he autographs the youngster's baseball.

Detroit outfielder Johnny Stone, a .327 hitter in 1931.

The Red Sox' Earl Webb, who set the major-league record with 67 doubles in 1931 while batting .333.

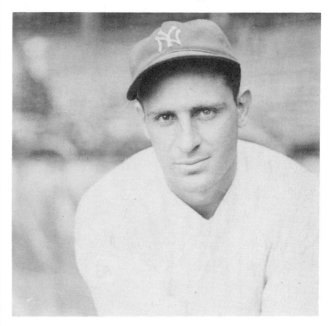

Ben Chapman. The aggressive, sharp-tongued Yankee outfielder batted .315 in 1931, drove in 122 runs, and led the league with 61 stolen bases, highest in the league between 1920 and 1968. (George Case also had 61, in 1943.)

Danny MacFayden, a 16-game winner for the Red Sox in 1931.

Washington third baseman Ossie Bluege has just nailed the Athletics' Max Bishop.

Eddie Morgan. The Cleveland first baseman hit .351 in 1931.

Vic Sorrell, whose 13 – 14 record was the best on the staff of the seventh-place Detroit Tigers in 1931.

Cubs first baseman Charlie Grimm, who took over the club from Rogers Hornsby in August and led them to the pennant.

1·9·3·2

In early August, Rogers Hornsby's Chicago Cubs were involved in a tight pennant race with the Pittsburgh Pirates when Hornsby was suddenly given the boot. Cubs president William Veeck (father of the colorful Bill Veeck, who in later years was to own the Cleveland Indians, St. Louis Browns, and Chicago White Sox) had had a series of disputes with his fiercely independent and outspoken skipper, culminating with Hornsby learning once again that the man who speaks last is the one who signs the checks (Rogers had undergone the same experience in St. Louis in 1926, which resulted in his being traded to the Giants after managing the Cardinals to the world championship).

Hornsby's replacement was the club's first baseman, Charlie Grimm, a man whose relaxed approach to the reins of management was in direct contrast to Hornsby's steely aloofness. Some of the Cub players thought Grimm was too casual and easygoing in exercising his authority, but, as second baseman Billy Herman recalled, "With that club it worked out okay."

The Cubs won the pennant by four games over the Pirates, who outhit the Chicagoans .285 to .278. The pennant winners were a blend of youth and experience. Rookie Herman and sophomore shortstop Billy Jurges gave the club its best keystone combination since the days of Joe Tinker and Johnny Evers a quarter century before, and another youngster, Stanley Hack, was beginning to break in at third base. When Jurges was sidelined with an injury late in the season, the team reached into the minor leagues and came up with the veteran Mark Koenig, a former Yankee, who filled in brilliantly for 33 games, batting .353. Koenig later was

to become involved, unwittingly, in the circumstances of a highly charged World Series.

The club still had some solid veterans of its 1929 pennant winners in outfielder Riggs Stephenson (at .324 the team's leading hitter), catcher Gabby Hartnett, outfielder Kiki Cuyler, and Grimm. Herman batted .314, Grimm .307, and outfielder Johnny Moore .305.

Another Cubs youngster was the league's best pitcher that year. Lon Warneke, a twenty-three-year-old right-hander, was 22–6, with the best earned-run average (2.37). Guy Bush was 19–11; Charlie Root, 15–10; and Pat Malone, 15–17. One writer described the Cubs starters as "perhaps the meanest staff of all time. Dusting off opposing batters was a routine part of their day's work." Herman described them as "the biggest bunch of headhunters you ever saw." And of course in those freewheeling days there was retaliation. "I think I must've had my tail in the batter's box as often as my feet," Herman said.

The second-place Pirates, who hit just 48 home runs, presented a lineup of contact hitters, six of whom struck out 26 or fewer times all year. Paul Waner (.341), Lloyd Waner (.333), and Pie Traynor (.329) were joined this year by another superlative rookie in shortstop Arky Vaughan, who broke in with a .318 average. Paul Waner had 62 doubles, which constituted a new National League record. Pittsburgh's ace was the talented left-hander Larry French, who was 18–16.

The biggest story in the National League in 1932 was the sudden retirement of John McGraw, on June 3. After 31 years of tumult and controversy, of triumph and bitterness, during which he had won 10 pennants, the

1·9·3·2

master of the New York Giants was stepping aside.

"He was the oldest fifty-nine-year-old man I ever knew," Fred Lindstrom said. "He was tired and he was angry. He resented it, but he knew it was time to go, and he went."

It was as if the fires that had burned within for three decades no longer had anything left to consume, and so John McGraw, who before the arrival of Babe Ruth had been the symbol of New York baseball, who had remained adamantly unyielding in a changing world, took his leave. He became a vice-president of the club but generally sat quietly through meetings. The field and the dugout had been his life, and without them he soon began to fade. He died on February 25, 1934.

McGraw's choice as his replacement (he had been given that courtesy by owner Charles Stoneham) was almost as surprising as the old man's departure: first baseman Bill Terry, with whom John J. had been carrying on a silent, sullen feud for years. But McGraw was first and foremost a baseball man, a New York Giant man, and in his judgment the best possible choice to succeed him was Terry. And so the thirty-three-year-old Terry, who that year batted .350 and had 225 hits, became only the Giants' second manager since 1903.

Along with Herman and Vaughan, another outstanding rookie entered the National League this year—the Cardinals' lanky, hard-throwing right-hander Jay Hanna (Dizzy) Dean. Dizzy was colorful, garrulous, magnificently self-confident, and at the age of twenty-one a canny and accomplished pitcher who poured in red-hot fast balls and broke off crackling curves with smooth, rippling, long-striding deliveries. A wit, a prankster, a cornpone philosopher, he was soon to become baseball's big-

gest drawing card and one of its magical names.

The world champion Cardinals plunged to seventh place in 1932, but it was hardly the fault of the new man, who immediately became the club ace with an 18–15 record and 191 league-leading strikeouts.

The Cardinals, in whose farm system the talent was beginning to bubble like freshly opened champagne, introduced another compelling youngster at the end of the season in twenty-year-old outfielder Joe Medwick, a strong, tough, surly kid from New Jersey who swung at bad balls and converted them into ringing line drives. Joe got into 26 games and announced himself with a .349 average.

The league's leading hitter was Brooklyn's Lefty O'Doul, who batted .368 to win his second batting title (Lefty had scraped the clouds with a .398 mark in 1929). The Dodgers also had the league's only other 20-game winner in left-hander Watty Clark (20–12). Chuck Klein continued to dent the fences in Baker Bowl, slamming 226 hits, most in the league, and tying New York's Mel Ott for the home run lead with 38. Chuck also led in stolen bases with 20, batted .348, and drove in 137 runs, and it all added up to a Most Valuable Player Award. Chuck's Phillies teammate Don Hurst was the RBI leader with 143. Along with this lustrous RBI total, the twenty-seven-year-old first baseman hit 24 home runs and batted .339. Two years later, however, his bat turned to Swiss cheese and he was gone from the major leagues.

With the Depression continuing to erode the economy, attendance at National League parks showed a steep decline. The Giants dropped from 812,163 admissions in 1931 to 484,868 in 1932. The Cardinals went from 608,535 to

1·9·3·2

279,219. Even the pennant-winning Cubs showed a drop off, from 1,086,422 to 974,688. Nevertheless, playing major-league baseball was still one of the country's surer and better-paying jobs. When he returned to his home in economically hard-hit Oklahoma after the season, Lloyd Waner said, "A lot of my friends came around to borrow money."

In the American league, the Yankees and Athletics reversed not only the order of their 1931 finishes, but almost their exact won-lost records as well. In 1931, the first-place A's had been 107–45, the second-place Yankees, 94–59. In 1932, the first-place Yankees were 107–47; the second place A's, 94–60.

For Joe McCarthy, it was the first of eight pennants he would bring to Yankee Stadium. Never really troubled during the summer, the Yankees won by 13 games over the A's and 14 over the Washington Senators, who finished strong, winning 34 of their final 46, which proved to be a portent for the 1933 season.

The Yankee lineup continued to be muscled by Babe Ruth and Lou Gehrig. Gehrig batted .349, hit 34 home runs, and drove in 151 runs. At the age of thirty-seven, Ruth was beginning to feel the subversions of time; but slowing down for Babe Ruth still meant a .341 batting average, 41 home runs, 137 runs batted in. Second baseman Tony Lazzeri drove in 113 runs and outfielder Ben Chapman, 107, while the remarkable Joe Sewell came to bat 503 times and struck out just 3 times.

Not even the mighty Grove could get the ball past the vigilant Sewell. "Sure, Lefty was tough to hit," Sewell said. "But I could pick up the ball the moment he turned it loose and I followed it right on in. And it came right on in. With Grove you didn't have much time."

This hard-hitting Yankee team went through the entire season without being shut out, something no other team before or since has achieved.

This time Yankee pitching was equal to the club's solid slugging, with Lefty Gomez at 24–7; Red Ruffing, 18–7; rookie Johnny Allen, 17–4; and George Pipgras, 16–9. Allen was a highly effective winning pitcher, but he was often swung about by violent inner tempests.

Reminiscing many years later, McCarthy recalled Johnny Allen.

"A good pitcher and a very tough kid," McCarthy said. "But he drank, and when he did he showed a mean streak."

The skipper did not have the same affection for Allen that he'd had for his Chicago Cub rowdies, nor did he have the same success in handling him, and a few years later Johnny was dispatched to Cleveland.

The Athletics led the league with a .290 batting average and hit 173 home runs, a new major-league record. The leading basher was Jimmie Foxx, who came right up to Babe Ruth's doorstep with 58 homers (Ruth had set the record with 60 in 1927), drove in 169 runs and batted .364, a year's work that earned him the MVP Award. Al Simmons dropped from .390 to .322, but his 151 RBIs kept his teammates spinning around the bases.

Lefty Grove was 25–10, and by the rarefied standards he had set the previous two years, this was something of a falling-off, though he did lead in ERA, his 2.84 mark the only one in the league under three. For the first time in his eight-year career, the Athletics' temperamental southpaw did not lead in strikeouts, his 188 whiffs being 2 less than leader Red Ruffing's.

The Washington Senators had the league's top winner in righthander Alvin Crowder,

1·9·3·2

known as "General," who was 26–13 (including a 15-game winning streak), followed by teammate Monte Weaver's 22–10.

Dale Alexander, traded by Detroit to Boston early in the season, won the batting championship with a .367 average, edging out Foxx by three points and costing Jimmie a Triple Crown. (Alexander and Harry Walker with the Cardinals and Phillies in 1947 are the only players ever to win batting championships while playing for two different teams in the same season.) The big first baseman played just five years in the majors (1929–33) and batted .331. Despite his potent bat, however, his slowness afoot and adventuresome ways with ground balls forced his departure from the big leagues at the age of thirty. Dale was a designated hitter born before his time.

Cleveland's Wes Ferrell was 23–13, making it four 20-game seasons in his first four years, a record that still stands. Wes was another tempestuous character, reacting to losing the way a cat reacts to a seat on a hot stove. Unlike Grove, however, who often would berate his teammates after suffering a low-score loss, Wes found fault only with himself.

"Wes was quite a fellow," his Cleveland manager Roger Peckinpaugh said. "I've seen him cutting up his glove with a pair of big black scissors after losing a tough one, or grinding his wristwatch into the floor with the heel of his shoe. His teammates would sit in front of their lockers watching him with open fascination."

Years later Ferrell could laugh at it all.

"Sure I did those things," he said. "What are you supposed to do after you lose, get up and sing a song? But one thing they said I did wasn't true—I never chewed up my glove. You ever taste a baseball glove?"

Wes's disposition wasn't helped by a game between Cleveland and Philadelphia on July 10. It was supposed to be a home game for the Athletics, but there was no Sunday ball in Philadelphia at that time, so the teams caught a sleeper to Cleveland. Always a careful man with a buck, Connie Mack reckoned there was no sense in going to the expense of bringing the whole team just for one game, so he left behind most of his pitchers. But fate punished Connie's frugality with an 18-inning game. His starter was driven from the mound in the first inning and right-hander Ed Rommel came in and was forced to work the rest of the way—a 17-inning relief stint, giving up 29 hits and 14 runs but still emerging as the winning pitcher as the A's won it, 18–17. Pitching the last 12 innings in relief for Cleveland was Ferrell, who remembered that he was beaten by a "bad-hop base hit." It was in this game that Cleveland shortstop Johnny Burnett set an all-time one-game record with nine hits (seven singles and two doubles).

It is an oft-told tale how the self-effacing Lou Gehrig was overshadowed first by the flamboyant Ruth and later by the elegantly majestic DiMaggio, and how on his greatest day—June 3, 1932—he was again deprived of stage center by the sudden retirement of John McGraw. On that day the Yankee first baseman put on a display of methodical high-powered hitting when he belted four home runs in a game against the Athletics, a game the Yankees won by a hefty 20–13 score. Gehrig, who hit his home runs consecutively in his first four at bats, was the first man in modern history to trot around the bases four times in one game. Nevertheless, the headline this day went to McGraw.

As had happened in the National League, American League attendance suffered a de-

1·9·3·2

cline in every city except New York, where the lure of Ruth was still strong. The eighth-place Boston Red Sox showed an almost fifty percent drop to 182,150, lowest in the club's history. Even with Ruth and a pennant-winning club, however, the Yankees still did not reach the million mark as they had done eight times in the prosperous, free-spending 1920s and again in 1930, settling for 962,320.

The World Series between the Cubs and Yankees was a noisy, raucous, ill-tempered affair that the Yankees swept in four. Despite some lusty hitting by Ruth and Gehrig, it would have been a forgettable set of games if not for what occurred at Wrigley Field in the fifth inning of the third game, when the name-calling and rancor between the two teams built into what stands as perhaps baseball's most mythic moment.

Relations between the teams had deteriorated even before a pitch was thrown, when the Cubs decided to vote Mark Koenig, their late-season, fill-in shortstop, a half share of Series money. Since Koenig was an ex-Yankee and had been very popular with his former teammates, the New Yorkers took offense and began calling the Cubs "cheapskates." The verbal warfare quickly escalated to vociferous name-calling, both in the newspapers and on the field. The Yankees won the first two games in New York and by the time the Series moved to Chicago the decibel level was at a screeching pitch, with the Cub fans now part of it.

At the center of all the shouting was Ruth. An accomplished bench jockey, Babe was also a prime target. By the time he came to bat in the fifth inning of the third game, not only invective was being hurled at him but fruits and vegetables from the stands. With Cub right-hander Charlie Root on the mound and the Chicago dugout in full vocal uproar, Ruth took two strikes and then made a pointing gesture. It is the import of this gesture that lies at the core of the legend of "the called shot." Was he pointing to Root or to the center field stands? Was he telling the roaring Chicago dugout he still had one strike left or was he announcing a home run? Whatever ambiguities there are about the prelude to this celebrated moment, there is no question about what happened when Ruth lashed his bat at the next pitch. The ball disappeared from the premises in a high, sizzling line, carrying an incredible distance in an incredibly short time.

The moment remains enwreathed in controversy. Root went to his grave angrily denying that Ruth had called a home run. Ruth from time to time stoked the story by saying he had, and at other times laughed it off as nonsense, which it probably was. In all likelihood the "called shot" was called only after the fact. Nevertheless, many a man tall and wise believes to this day that Babe Ruth predicted his home run in Chicago. The episode has by now drifted into folklore and from that mellow realm the story that is too good not to be true can no longer be retrieved.

Jimmie Foxx.

Born in Sudlersville, Maryland, on October 22, 1907, Jimmie Foxx came to the big leagues at the age of seventeen with the Philadelphia Athletics in 1925, a smiling, apple-cheeked youngster who was still developing one of the most impressive physiques ever seen in the major leagues.

Jimmie's hallmark—his awesome power—was in evidence early. By 1928, his first full season, his ability to dispatch a ball for great distances was already being compared to Ruth's; indeed, he was known as "the right-handed Ruth," which, as one writer pointed out, "was all you needed to know."

Jimmie's explosive home runs became the yardsticks all around the league, to the point where White Sox pitcher Ted Lyons said, "If somebody points out to you where Foxx hit, believe it, no matter how incredible the distance."

Ted Williams described Foxx as "next to Joe DiMaggio, the greatest ballplayer I ever saw." Jimmie's versatility was unusual for a power hitter; he came up as a catcher, then played third base before being switched permanently to first base. As late as 1940, when the need arose, he caught 42 games for the Red Sox.

Jimmie's heavy pounding began in earnest in 1929, when he hit 33 home runs, the first of

12 consecutive seasons of 30 or more (the major league record), during which he hit over 40 five times, including 50 in 1938 and his peak of 58 in 1932, still the record for right-handed hitters (tied with Hank Greenberg).

In 1929, Jimmie began a string of 13 straight years of over 100 runs batted in, a record he shares with Lou Gehrig. Four times he drove in over 150 runs in a season, with a personal high of 175 in 1938 (only Hack Wilson, Gehrig, and Greenberg have done better).

Three times the American League's Most Valuable Player as well as a Triple Crown winner, Foxx hit consistently for high average, winning two batting titles and posting a .325 lifetime average. Swinging against such heavy competitors as Ruth, Gehrig, Greenberg, and DiMaggio during his career, Foxx led in home runs four times, RBIs three times, and slugging five times. In three World Series he hit .344.

Jimmie was a heavy drinker and this probably contributed to a premature decline in his output. He was thirty-four years old when the Red Sox waived him to the Cubs in 1942. At this point the banner years of Jimmie Foxx were now history. He finished up in 1945 with the Philadelphia Phillies, for whom he hit the last of his 534 career home runs. At the time of his retirement, in 1945, Foxx was second to Ruth on the all-time home-run list.

The man known as "The Beast" (for his imposing physique) and "Double-X" died on July 21, 1967, at the age of fifty-nine.

Billy Jurges, shortstop on the 1932 pennant-winning Chicago Cubs.

Billy Herman. The young second baseman played his first full season for the Cubs in 1932, batting .314.

Dodger infielder Joe Stripp, a steady .300 hitter throughout most of the 1930s.

The Cubs' Gabby Hartnett, generally considered the National League's premier catcher in the 1930s.

Lon Warneke, who was 22–6 for the pennant-winning Cubs in 1932.

Dizzy Dean.

Pittsburgh shortstop Arky Vaughan. A rookie in 1932, he batted .318.

Brooklyn's Lefty O'Doul. His .368 batting average was the best in the National League in 1932.

Pitching in his 20th big-league season, Yankee left-hander Herb Pennock was 9–5, helping the club to the pennant.

Lou Gehrig *(left)* and Babe Ruth.

Yankee right-hander Red Ruffing, who was 18–7 in 1932.

The tempestuous Johnny Allen. In 1932 the rookie right-hander helped the Yankees to the pennant with a 17–4 record.

Bill Dickey, in the opinion of many the greatest of all catchers.

You're peering into the sharp eyes of Yankee third baseman Joe Sewell. In 1932 he went to bat 503 times and struck out just 3 times.

The Babe coming to terms in an alfresco signing in St. Petersburg, Florida, in the spring of 1932. Ruth is flanked by Yankee owner Jacob Ruppert *(left)* and manager Joe McCarthy.

Al Lopez, who for years held the record for most games caught in the major leagues. In 1932 he was with Brooklyn.

Jimmie Foxx.

Lefty Gomez, the Yankee ace in 1932. The fast baller was 24–7.

The Giants' Mel Ott, the National League home-run champ in 1932.

Brooklyn's Watson Clark, who was 20–12 in 1932.

Monte Weaver, who was 22–10 for Washington in 1932.

A quartet of New York Giant infielders in the spring of 1932. *Left to right:* third baseman Johnny Vergez, short stop Travis Jackson, third baseman Hughie Critz, first baseman Bill Terry.

Don Hurst, the National League's RBI leader in 1932 with 143. It was the best year the Phillies first baseman ever had.

Cubs right-hander Charlie Root, who in the 1932 World Series became an imperishable adjunct to the Babe Ruth legend.

Dodger manager Max Carey *(center)* with a couple of veterans whose careers were winding down: Hack Wilson *(left)* and George Kelly. Hack drove in 123 runs for the Dodgers in 1932. It was his last productive season.

The American League's biggest winner in 1932 was Washington's Alvin Crowder, who was 26–13.

Dale Alexander, the American League batting champion in 1932.

Cleveland shortstop Johnny Burnett, who rapped out a record nine hits in an extra-inning game.

Doc Cramer, one of the steadiest players of his era. With the A's in 1932, Doc batted .336.

Earl Averill, one of the most popular players in Cleveland Indian history.

In the early 1930s Cleveland's handsome pitcher Wes Ferrell was invited out to Hollywood to test for the movies. This picture is from a series of stills taken at the time. Hollywood was interested, but Wes decided the movies weren't for him. "I told them I had a job," the Indians' 20-game winner said.

Guy Bush, who was 19–11 for the pennant-winning Cubs in 1932.

Dick Bartell, one of the National League's top shortstops during the 1930s. He batted .308 for the Phillies in 1932.

St. Louis Browns first baseman Jack Burns. He batted .305 in 1932, his best year in the big leagues.

Four key members of the 1932 National League pennant winners. *Left to right:* Kiki Cuyler, Gabby Hartnett, Riggs Stephenson, and Charlie Grimm.

Bump Hadley.

In his 19th big-league season, the White Sox' Sam Jones was 10–15 in 1932. Sam pitched on until 1935.

Harpo Marx is the tour guide for a group of visitors to a studio back lot in Hollywood. The visitors, all employees of the New York Giants, are *(left to right):* Freddie Lindstrom, coach Dave Bancroft, Travis Jackson, and Bill Terry.

In this spring training picture Rogers Hornsby, then managing the Cubs, is flanked by young third baseman Stan Hack *(left)* and outfielder Danny Taylor.

Right-hander George Blaeholder, who led the Browns' staff in 1932 with a 14–14 record.

Outfielder Smead Jolley had a strong bat but a weak glove. He split the 1932 season between the White Sox and Red Sox, batting .312 and driving in 106 runs.

Philadelphia Athletics shortstop Eric McNair. His 47 doubles led the American League in 1932.

Clint Brown, who was 15–12 for the Indians in 1932.

Dick Porter, nicknamed "Twitchy." The Cleveland outfielder batted .308 in 1932.

White Sox manager Lew Fonseca.

Freddie Fitzsimmons, a 16-game winner for the Giants in 1933.

1·9·3·3

It took just one year for Bill Terry to justify John McGraw's judgment. In 1933, the Giant club that had finished an uninspiring sixth the year before followed Terry's quiet leadership to a pennant, five games ahead of Pittsburgh. With a .322 batting average, the skipper was the only man on the pennant winners to clear the .300 mark. Mel Ott drove in 103 runs, good enough to rank third in the league in this year of moderated hitting.

The Giants' .263 team average was bettered by five other clubs in the league, but no one could match Terry's three aces, Carl Hubbell, Hal Schumacher, and Freddie Fitzsimmons, whose fine work was supported by a pair of veteran right-handed relievers, the forty-two-year-old Dolf Luque and the thirty-five-year-old Hi Bell.

For Hubbell, it was the beginning of a run of five remarkable seasons, during which he earned the nickname "King Carl" and a place among the greatest of baseball's left-handers. Hubbell was quiet, colorless, and exquisitely efficient. Throwing a maddeningly elusive screwball over which he had masterful control, the Giant ace put up a 23–12 record that included ten shutouts and a 1.66 earned-run average, both league-leading figures. He was voted the National League's Most Valuable Player in 1933.

Schumacher—inevitably "Prince Hal" to Hubbell's "King Carl"—was 19–12. A right-hander with a sinking fast ball, Schumacher pitched seven shutouts, giving the Giants' two top pitchers 17 blankers between them, more than any other team in the league. Fitzsimmons, a knuckle baller, was 16–11.

On July 2, Hubbell turned in one of the most shimmering artistic performances in baseball history, a 1–0, 18-inning victory over the Cardinals at the Polo Grounds, during which he yielded just six hits and no walks. (The idea of allowing any pitcher, much less an ace, to go 18 innings in one day seems positively medieval today. Did this effort deplete Hubbell? Hardly: shortly after, on July 13, he began a string of 46 consecutive scoreless innings, which remained the National League record until broken by Don Drysdale in 1968.)

Pittsburgh earned high marks for consistency in 1933. The year before, they had finished second with an 86–68 record and .285 batting average; in 1933 they finished second with an 87–67 record and .285 batting average. The Pirates had five .300 hitters in the lineup in Arky Vaughan, Paul Waner, Fred Lindstrom, Tony Piet, and Pie Traynor. This club didn't hit with very much power—they had just 39 home runs all season—but neither did they strike out very often, just 334 times.

The Pirates outhit the Giants by 22 points, a fairly substantial margin, but Bill Terry's pitching staff, lead by Hubbell, had a 2.71 ERA compared to Pittsburgh's 3.27. Left-hander Larry French (18–13) was again the ace of the staff.

The National League had a Triple Crown winner this year in Philadelphia's Chuck Klein. Swinging a heavy bat for the fifth year in a row, Klein batted .368, hit 28 home runs, and drove in 120 runs.

"Chuck was a very nice man," Fred Lindstrom, a teammate of Klein's on the 1935 Cubs, said. "And that was a good thing, because he had the kind of strength that could tear telephone books in half. But because he was so

1·9·3·3

strong and easygoing, some of the guys enjoyed playing practical jokes on him. I suppose there was some kind of thrill in it. I remember one time somebody—I don't recall who it was—slipped into the clubhouse during a game and with a pair of scissors snipped off the sleeves of Chuck's white shirt, right up to the shoulders. Later, when the game was over and Chuck had showered, he started getting dressed and put that shirt on and just stood there dumbfounded, his bare arms hanging down. He looked like he was wearing a white vest."

Klein had now played five full years in the major leagues and produced 200 or more hits in each of them, an achievement no other player before or since has equaled. Including the partial season he had in 1928, Klein's batting average at this point was .359. After the 1933 season, the Phillies dealt their star to the Cubs for cash and players, and Chuck was never the same devastating hitter again. A combination of injuries and the loss of Baker Bowl's beckoning borders turned him from a superstar into an average player.

In addition to Hubbell, there were three other 20-game winners in the league this year: Chicago's Guy Bush (20–12), Boston's Ben Cantwell (20–10), and St. Louis's Dizzy Dean (20–18). Dizzy was now a bona fide star as well as a burgeoning personality. For the second year in a row he was the strikeout champ, with 199, including a new major-league-record 17 against the Cubs on July 30. Not just Dean but the entire Cardinal ball club was beginning to draw attention, despite a fifth-place finish.

Frankie Frisch had replaced Gabby Street as Cardinal manager in July and the club seemed to play with more zest after that. Joe Medwick in his first full season batted .306; Pepper Mar-

tin, a .316 hitter, continued to play in his rugged, irrepressible style, as if, as one teammate put it, "He had electricity running up his ass"; and an early-season acquisition from Cincinnati, Leo Durocher, was now at shortstop, and nobody was slicker of glove nor sharper of tongue.

For Bill McKechnie's Boston Braves there was a refreshing moral victory as the club finished fourth, their highest slot since a fourth-place windup in 1921. The team's big gun was outfielder Wally Berger, a good hitter doomed to spend his best years with losing clubs. Wally batted .313 in 1933 and finished second to Klein in home runs (27) and runs batted in (106).

A good example of the occasional untrustworthiness of statistics was given by the record this year of Paul Derringer. Traded in early May by the Cardinals to the Reds in the deal that brought Durocher to St. Louis, the big right-hander labored in unremitting frustration through the summer, ending with a horrendous 7–27 record despite a respectable 3.30 ERA. Nevertheless, Derringer, who pitched for a weak last-place club that year, had his admirers, among them Paul Waner, who stated that "only Hubbell and Dean and maybe Warneke are tougher to hit against."

The year saw the introduction of a new American sports institution, the All-Star Game. Initially conceived as a one-time-only pageant, the game, played on July 6 at Chicago's Comiskey Park, was a "natural" that immediately caught the public imagination and became an annual midseason extravaganza. The first All-Star Game, with the squads managed by Connie Mack and John McGraw (out of retirement for the occasion), was won by the American League 4–2 on a Babe Ruth home run.

1·9·3·3

Years later Bill Hallahan, the Cardinal left-hander who started for the National League, recalled the aura of baseball's greatest player.

"Here we were," Hallahan said, "the pick of the National League, every one of us an all-star, a big shot. But when Babe Ruth came to the plate we were like a bunch of kids, couldn't keep our eyes off of him. He didn't disappoint us, either. Sure, I served up his home run, but I just had to shake my head and smile. That was the Babe; he was supposed to do that."

The Washington Senators, who had finished the 1932 season at a gallop, kept the momentum going the following year and won the pennant. The Senators moved the Yankees out of first place in June and maintained a winning pace the rest of the way, finishing seven games ahead of Joe McCarthy's club.

The galvanizing force behind the Senators was their twenty-six-year-old manager-shortstop Joe Cronin. Cronin, who was also the son-in-law of Washington owner Clark Griffith, batted .309 and drove in 118 runs. Hard-nosed rather than graceful in the field, the skipper was considered one of the toughest clutch hitters of his time.

Though they hit just 60 home runs (less than half the totals of second-place New York and third-place Philadelphia), the Senators scattered around enough base hits to lead the league with a .287 team batting average. Outfielder Heinie Manush led the way at .336; first baseman Joe Kuhel, .322; and second baseman Buddy Myer, .302. At third base was Ossie Bluege, whom old-timers said was as snappy with the glove as any third baseman ever. Outfielders Goose Goslin, Fred Schulte, and catcher Luke Sewell rounded out an extremely solid ball club.

"One very important factor that year," Bluege said, "was we were blessed with good health. As I recall, we were virtually injury free." Bluege was correct—the fewest games played by any regular was Myer's 131.

Washington pitching was topped by three veterans having excellent years. Alvin Crowder, a 26-game winner in 1932, led the staff with a 24–15 record, followed by southpaws Earl Whitehill (22–8) and Lefty Stewart (15–6), backed up by some good relief pitching from Jack Russell.

It was, said catcher Luke Sewell, a great year to be playing ball in Washington and for Clark Griffith, a notorious skinflint whom many players nevertheless felt genuine affection for. Sewell recalled a scene after Cronin had driven in a couple of crucial ninth-inning runs against the Yankees, with Griffith sitting in a box seat next to the Washington dugout.

"You should have seen Griff. He raised up in his seat and began waving his hat. Then I guess he just couldn't contain his excitement and jumped right over that low railing onto the field. Well, Griff had a bad back, and as he went over the railing, his back gave away and down he went, still yelling, still waving his hat, still smoking his cigar, as the runners were going around the bases. We all jumped out of the dugout, not knowing what to do. Here are men crossing the plate, and there's the club owner lying there howling with both pain and delight. You never saw so much confusion in your life."

Yankee pitching fell off in 1933 and, combined with the decline of Ruth, helped confine the world champions to second place. Lefty Gomez was 16–10 and Johnny Allen, 15–7, while Red Ruffing slipped to 9–14.

Ruth was falling from such sublime heights

1·9·3·3

that his 34 home runs, 103 runs batted in, and .301 batting average were seen as the coming of twilight for the great man. Lou Gehrig remained sturdy with 32 homers, 139 RBIs, and a .334 average, and Bill Dickey and Ben Chapman gave the New Yorkers four .300 hitters. Joe Sewell, in his final big-league year, went to bat 524 official times and struck out in only 4 of them.

Bedeviled by declining attendance, high salaries, a bleeding on the stock market, and the national economic situation in general, Connie Mack began the dismantling of the superb team that had won pennants in 1929, '30, and '31. Outfielders Mule Haas and Al Simmons and infielder Jimmy Dykes were the first to go, dispatched to the White Sox for $100,000.

Connie still had Grove, who won 24 and lost 8, and Jimmie Foxx, who won the Triple Crown with 48 home runs, 163 RBIs, and a .356 batting average, winning handily in each category. Jimmie's tripart championship slugging, matched by Chuck Klein, gave Philadelphia the rarity of two Triple Crown winners in the same city in the same year.

After the season, Mack picked up another $100,000 when he sent Mickey Cochrane to Detroit, where the great catcher was also signed to manage. While Connie moved in some fine young talent in third baseman Pinky Higgins and outfielders Doc Cramer and Bob Johnson, there would be no more pennants for the old man, though he remained steadfastly at the helm of his Athletics for another 17 years, retiring in 1950 at the age of eighty-seven.

On August 3, the Yankees were finally shut out after a record span of 308 games, the equivalent of exactly two full seasons. The man who hung the goose eggs around McCarthy's club was, perhaps inevitably, Lefty Grove, who claimed he never feared Ruth or Gehrig "or any of those free swingers." Instead, "It was those little guys, like that Joe Sewell, who gave me fits. Hard as I threw it, he'd just reach out with his bat and, *ping,* a little single over the shortstop's head.

Later in August, on the 17th, Gehrig, seemingly programmed for brute consistency and unshakable endurance, broke Everett Scott's major-league record for consecutive games by playing in his 1,308th straight game, dating back to 1925. The Yankees' Iron Man still had another 822 straight lineups to crash before terminal illness removed him from the game in May 1939.

Early in the season, Washington's Ossie Bluege was sidelined for injuries and the Senators brought up young Cecil Travis as a temporary replacement. Travis, a nineteen-year-old contact hitter who would soon be a .300-hitting shortstop for Washington, set a rookie record when he broke in May 16 with five hits in a 12-inning game. When Bluege returned a few weeks later, however, Travis was returned to the minors, probably wondering what a fellow had to do.

Terry's Giants wiped out the Senators in five games in the World Series, with Hubbell winning twice. In 20 innings, King Carl gave up no earned runs. An Earl Whitehill shutout in Game 3 was Washington's only victory.

The Boston Red Sox, long one of baseball's more moribund franchises, had a new, rich, and energetically determined owner in Tom Yawkey, who came into the picture saying he was not going "to mess with a loser." Putting his resolve into action, Yawkey that December gave Connie Mack $125,000 and a couple of players for Grove, Rube Walberg, and second

1·9·3·3

baseman Max Bishop. As much fan as owner, Yawkey would spend freely on behalf of his team over the next dozen years, but was doomed more times than not to find it in the path of the Yankee steamroller. It wasn't until 1946 that the champagne popped in the Red Sox clubhouse.

The infield of the 1933 Boston Red Sox. *Left to right:* first baseman Dale Alexander, second baseman Johnny Hodapp, shortstop Rabbit Warstler, and third baseman-manager Marty McManus.

Carl Hubbell.

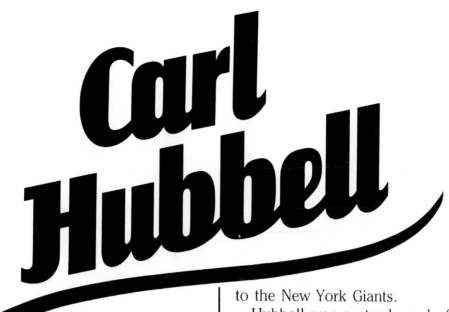

Carl Hubbell

Carl Hubbell, the talented, poker-faced left-handed ace of the New York Giants in the 1930s, was born in Carthage, Missouri, on June 22, 1903. When he was four years old, the family moved to Meeker, Oklahoma, where the youngster grew up on a pecan farm. It was upon these quiet stretches of Oklahoma farmland that Hubbell learned to play and to love baseball.

Initially signed by the Detroit Tigers in the 1920s, Hubbell soon came to the attention of the manager, Ty Cobb. Cobb disapproved of the eccentric pitch the young left-hander threw and ordered him to drop it from his repertory.

Hubbell, however, needed the pitch, since his fast ball and curve were average at best. But Cobb's order prevailed, and Hubbell went back to the minor leagues, where, deprived of the major weapon in his arsenal, he was little more than a mediocre pitcher. Within a few years the Tigers gave up on him and let him go.

Hubbell was pitching in the Texas League in 1928—throwing his screwball again—when a Giant scout spotted him and in a highly laudatory phone call to New York urged John McGraw to buy the twenty-five-year-old left-hander. So it was in midsummer 1928 that Carl Hubbell, destined to become the club's greatest pitcher since Christy Mathewson, reported to the New York Giants.

Hubbell was a steady and efficient winner his first five years in New York, running off win totals of 10, 18, 17, 14, and 18. And then in 1933 he began a five-year skein of a different order, one that was eventually to elevate him to his place among the most remarkable of pitchers. It wasn't just his winning totals—23, 21, 23, 26, 22—that caught the imagination of baseball fans, but the fact that he was throwing that slyly tantalizing screwball, over which he had near absolute mastery. It made him unique among pitchers.

"His control of that thing was so good," Cubs third baseman Stan Hack said, "that sometimes he'd deliberately fall behind in the count, knowing that you'd be swinging, and then throw you the screwball and let you bounce it into an infielder's glove."

Hubbell will always be remembered most prominently for his five-strikeout performance in the 1934 All-Star Game, but along with that larger-than-life exhibition he has his five 20-game seasons, his two MVP Awards, three ERA titles, and lifetime record of 253–154.

"I faced that screwball many times," Cincinnati first baseman Frank McCormick said, "and I can tell you exactly what the experience was like: there it was, and there it wasn't. You never took a more confident swing than the one you took at a Hubbell screwball, and you always walked back to the bench thinking the same thing: 'How the hell did *that* happen?'"

Giants second baseman Hughie Critz.

Goose Goslin, part of the Washington outfield in 1933.

Hal Schumacher, who won 19 for the pennant-winning Giants in 1933.

Jo-Jo Moore, steady as a rock for the Giants throughout the 1930s.

Carl Hubbell.

Mel Ott.

Travis Jackson, veteran Giant shortstop.

Washington catcher Luke Sewell.

Joe Cronin. Washington's shortstop-manager batted .309 and led the league with 45 doubles.

Earl Whitehill, Washington's ace left-hander in 1933. Earl was 22–8.

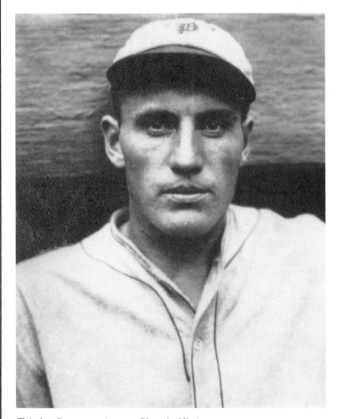

Triple Crown winner Chuck Klein.

Dodger fireballer Van Mungo. He was 16–15 in 1933.

Joe Kuhel, first baseman for the pennant-winning Senators in 1933. Joe batted .322, the highest average of his 18-year career.

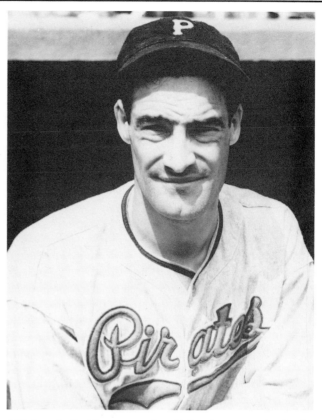

Pittsburgh first baseman Gus Suhr. At one point in the 1930s he played in 822 consecutive games, which at the time was the National League record.

Goose Goslin taking his rips.

Philadelphia Athletics right-hander Roy Mahaffey.

Mule Haas, who had been dealt by the Athletics to the White Sox as Connie Mack began breaking up his championship team.

The Athletics' young third baseman Pinky Higgins, a .314 hitter in 1933.

A solid slugger for the Athletics throughout the 1930s, outfielder Bob Johnson had 21 home runs in 1933.

Joe McCarthy *(left)* and Babe Ruth. They didn't much care for each other.

Twenty-two-year-old Dixie Walker with the Yankees in 1933.

Dodger right-hander Walter (Boom-Boom) Beck. Boom-Boom was 12–20 for the sixth-place Dodgers in 1933.

Lefty Stewart. The former Browns ace was 15–6 for the Senators in 1933.

A couple of veteran first basemen hanging on with the Dodgers in 1933: Del Bissonette *(left)* and Joe Judge.

A familiar figure in an unfamiliar uniform: Cleveland manager Walter Johnson. Walter had spent 25 years in a Washington uniform as player and manager.

Oral Hildebrand, ace of the Cleveland staff in 1933 with a 16–11 record.

Boston's third baseman-manager Marty McManus is flanked by new Red Sox owner Tom Yawkey *(left)* and general manager Eddie Collins.

Washington second baseman Buddy Myer.

The managers for the first All-Star Game: Connie Mack *(left)* for the American League and John McGraw for the National. McGraw came out of retirement for the occasion.

Part of the starting staff of the pennant-winning 1933 Washington Senators. *Left to right:* Alvin Crowder, Monte Weaver, and Earl Whitehill.

Heinie Manush, one of baseball's most consistent hitters. Heinie, who had a .333 lifetime average, batted .336 for the pennant-winning Washington Senators in 1933.

Three American League All-Stars. *Left to right:* Babe Ruth, Al Simmons, and Earl Averill.

An aerial view of Washington's Griffith Stadium.

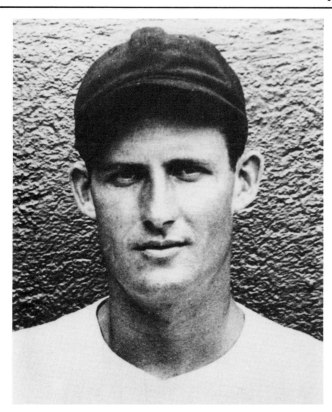

Right-hander Jack Russell, who worked very successfully out of the bull pen for the Senators in 1933.

Outfielder Roy Johnson, brother of the Athletics' Bob. Roy was a .313 hitter for the Red Sox in 1933.

Riggs Stephenson *(left)* and Babe Herman of the Chicago Cubs. They are at the team's Catalina Island spring camp in 1933.

Sammy West, who played the outfield for the Browns and Senators throughout the 1930s, generally batting over .300.

Catcher Rick Ferrell, who split the 1933 season between the Browns and Red Sox.

Al Simmons.

Boston Braves right-hander Fred Frankhouse, who was 16–15 in 1933.

The White Sox' perennial .300-hitting shortstop Luke Appling.

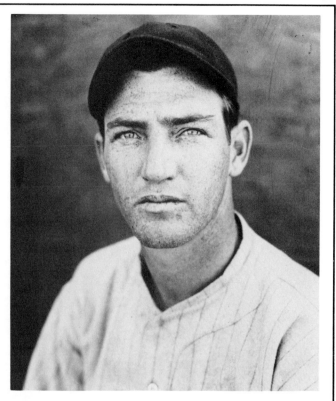

Pepper Martin. He batted .316 in 1933 and led the National League in stolen bases with 26.

Detroit's rookie right-hander Schoolboy Rowe.

President Franklin D. Roosevelt delivering a ceremonial first pitch during the 1933 World Series. On the President's left are Giants manager Bill Terry and Senators owner Clark Griffith.

Rip Collins being greeted at home plate by Joe Medwick after homering.

1·9·3·4

Although generally well liked by his players, Giants manager Bill Terry was never taken warmly to heart by the Polo Grounds fans. There was a natural aloofness and businesslike quality to the Terry personality that did not evoke affection. The last thing anyone ever expected from Bill Terry, who was tersely cordial with the press, was a wisecrack. As far as the record shows, he made only one, and that one proved sufficient unto a lifetime.

In the spring of 1934, the Giant manager was discussing the National League teams with a group of writers when one of them asked, "What about Brooklyn?" In response, Terry stepped out of character and attempted a bit of levity.

"Brooklyn?" he said. "Is Brooklyn still in the league?"

Harmless enough, but not in the always highly charged atmosphere of Dodger–Giant baseball, and particularly galling to Dodger fans whose team had not prospered lately, fans who thrived on frenetic loyalty; and even more galling because this sally of wit had dropped from the lips not just of Bill Terry, manager of the despised Giants, but the especially despised *world champion* Giants. In an adaptation of the old let-sleeping-dogs-lie wisdom, it was inadvisable to allow condescending humor to roll down the slopes onto the backs of the less fortunate.

According to Dodger catcher Al Lopez, Terry's remark "had never bothered the Dodger players any, but it seemed to have rankled the fans." And if there didn't seem to be much justice in the land in the Depression year of 1934, a big swath of it cut through the Polo Grounds on the last two days of the season.

The Giants had spent most of the summer in first place, but in mid-August the Cardinals got hot and played to a 33–12 record from then on, steadily chipping away at the Giant lead, finally catching Terry's team as the season went into its final two days. With the clubs tied with identical 93–58 records, the Cardinals had two games scheduled with the last-place Reds in St. Louis, while the Giants were at home with the sixth-place Dodgers. For Dodger fans, another dismal season could suddenly be redeemed, for the only thing sweeter for a Dodger fan than winning the pennant was to prevent the Giants from doing the same, and with Terry's infamous wisecrack still ringing in their ears, the Brooklyn partisans came roaring to the Polo Grounds for those final two games.

"They were running up and down the aisles waving banners and yelling and really cheering us on," Lopez said.

On Saturday, the Dodgers' Van Lingle Mungo beat the Giants 5–1 while the Cardinals were winning in St. Louis, and the next day the Dodgers (who were managed by Casey Stengel) again beat the Giants, making the Cardinals' final victory unnecessary.

If Bill Terry made one wisecrack that year, then Dizzy Dean probably made thousands. It was the year of Dizzy—of both Dean brothers, in fact. The Cardinals ace was joined this year by his younger brother Paul, an exceptionally hard-throwing right-hander. Inappropriately nicknamed "Daffy," Paul was a personality contrast to his brother, being a shy young man of few words. For Dizzy it was his mountaintop year of glory, a 30–7 record and the Most Valuable Player Award. This glittering year made the buoyantly uninhibited Dean baseball's

1·9·3·4

biggest drawing card. He became, along with Babe Ruth, the country's most popular athlete, a fresh and zestful breeze through the doldrums of a dispirited and demoralized nation. Shrewdly cornpone and homespun, he boastfully predicted his shutouts, called himself "The Great One," and got away with it all, because the press not only liked him but needed him, too. Dizzy Dean seemed to be one of the few optimists abroad in the land in 1934, an embodiment and upholder of old truths and values.

Between them, the Deans won 49 games (Dizzy had predicted 50 in the spring), Paul turning in a 19–11 record. The brothers reached a peak of efficiency in a doubleheader against the Dodgers at Ebbets Field on September 21. In the opener Dizzy blanked the Dodgers on three hits, and in the nightcap Paul upstaged his brother by tossing a 3–0 no-hitter.

They were "The Gashouse Gang," these Cardinals, managed by Frankie Frisch, who endured a summer of pranks and practical jokes concocted by Dizzy, first baseman Rip Collins, and third baseman Pepper Martin. They were a hard-playing, "dirty-uniformed" team, and they included the burgeoning Joe Medwick (.319), catcher Spud Davis (.300), outfielder Ernie Orsatti (.300), and shortstop Leo Durocher. Skipper Frisch batted .305, and Collins drove in 128 runs, led with 35 home runs (tying Mel Ott), and batted .333. With five .300 hitters in the lineup, the Cardinals topped the league with a .288 batting average.

Bill Terry, always sharper of bat than of wit, hit .354 for the Giants, outfielder Jo-Jo Moore was at .331 and Ott hit .326. Mel, in addition to tying for the home-run lead, was at the top of the league with 135 RBIs. With his uncanny ability to pull the ball, Ott was always lethal in the Polo Grounds with its 257-foot right-field foul line.

The Giants had Hubbell at 23–10; Hal Schumacher, 21–12; and Freddie Fitzsimmons, 18–14—a strong mound trio, but not enough to offset the Deans, particularly with Dizzy winning 23 more than he lost. Hubbell's 2.30 ERA was the best in the league.

Lon Warneke, 22–10 for the third-place Cubs, was the league's only other big winner.

Pittsburgh's Paul Waner won his second batting crown with a .362 average, also leading in hits with 217. Paul, a noted tippler, once served as a colorful illustration for Casey Stengel. Asked to define "big league," Casey said, "To me, 'big league' is Paul Waner lining one into the open spaces and whirling around the bases and sliding into third without breaking the bottle in his hip pocket."

The site of the All-Star Game that year was the Polo Grounds and the occasion produced one of baseball's unforgettable performances. The starting pitcher for the National League was Carl Hubbell. Working in his home park, the Giant ace was confronted by an awesome array of hitters. The first two men to face him, Charlie Gehringer and Heinie Manush, reached base, and now the hometown favorite had to contend with Babe Ruth, Lou Gehrig, and Jimmie Foxx, to be followed by Al Simmons and Joe Cronin.

Working methodically and with exquisite precision, Hubbell baffled and dazzled the three greatest power hitters in baseball, striking out Ruth, Gehrig, and Foxx in order, and walked off the mound to a tremendous ovation. But King Carl was not through; he opened the top of the second inning by striking out Simmons and Cronin, giving him five in a row. Bill Dickey broke the string with a single, but then

1·9·3·4

Hubbell whiffed his counterpart, Lefty Gomez, giving him six strikeouts in two innings.

Much to the regret of National League fans, Hubbell pitched just three innings, leaving with a 4–0 lead. His successors were unable to keep the American Leaguers in check, however, and the American League won for the second year in a row, 9–7.

"Cochrane was the spark that ignited us. He was an inspirational leader."

That was Hank Greenberg, describing Detroit's new catcher-manager, who joined the team in 1934 and led them to the first Tiger pennant since 1909. And Mickey Cochrane was indeed an igniter and an inspiration. The man described as being "tough as flint" by one teammate, whose appetite for winning was near insatiable, and who was described as "fiery" so often that we must disbelieve it at our peril was indeed the crucial final piece that brought a strong Tiger team together into a compact unity.

As Cochrane had teamed in Philadelphia with two of baseball's all-time great players in Foxx and Simmons, so did he match up in Detroit with first baseman Greenberg and second baseman Charlie Gehringer. Big Henry was in just his second full season and at the age of twenty-three was establishing himself as a major powerhouse. In 1934 he hit 26 home runs, drove in 139 runs, and batted .339, and he was just warming up.

Those who saw Gehringer in his prime say there simply cannot have been a better second baseman ever. Pleasantly reticent, he was known as "The Quiet Man," and for his seamlessly fine defensive play and pure hitting he was also called "The Mechanical Man." "He says hello in the spring and goodbye in the

fall," one of his teammates said, "and in between bats .350."

"He had the most placid disposition you could imagine," Greenberg said of Charlie, "always the same no matter what happened. And as far as being the perfect ballplayer, well, I put him in a class with DiMaggio, as far as being able to do everything and do it with grace and style. I can't imagine Joe or Charlie ever perspiring on a ball field."

In 1934, the thirty-one-year-old Gehringer, who had joined the Tigers in 1924 when Ty Cobb was still managing, batted .356 and drove in 127 runs. Four Tigers knocked in 100 or more runs that year, and three of them were in the infield, shortstop Billy Rogell being the other. Third baseman Marv Owen, a .317 batter, drove in 96 runs.

Goose Goslin, part of Washington's 1933 pennant-winning outfield, had been traded to Detroit the previous December, just in time to head into another World Series. The Goose, now in his 14th year, was still an extremely dangerous hitter, batting .305 and piling up 100 RBIs. Outfielder Jo-Jo White checked in at .313, while Cochrane was at .320. As a unit, the Tigers had a .300 batting average, tops in the league.

The Detroit staff featured a quartet of right-handers: Schoolboy Rowe (24–8), Tommy Bridges (22–11), Fred Marberry (15–5), and Eldon Auker (15–7). Rowe's superb season included a 16-game winning streak from June 15 to August 25, tying him with Smokey Joe Wood, Walter Johnson, and Lefty Grove for the league record. Trying to establish a new mark on August 29, Rowe was raked by the Athletics, 13–5.

In fifth place in early June, the Tigers began a move that enabled them to overtake the first-place Yankees at the end of July and thereafter

1·9·3·4

were never headed, winning the pennant by seven games.

The Yankee pitching was actually more efficient than Detroit's, Joe McCarthy's staff finishing with a 3.75 earned-run average to the Tigers' 4.06, thanks primarily to Lefty Gomez's league-leading 2.33. If there had been a Cy Young Award in those years, it would no doubt have gone to the Yankee left-hander, who had the best year of his career, compiling a 26–5 record, leading in complete games (25), strikeouts (158), shutouts (6), as well as ERA. Red Ruffing followed Lefty with a 19–11 record.

For the second year in a row the American League had a Triple Crown winner; this time it was Lou Gehrig, the Yankee first baseman pounding his way to three-cornered glory with 49 home runs, 165 runs batted in, and a .363 batting average. (In spite of this thundering output, the Most Valuable Player Award went to Cochrane.)

Hurting the Yankees this year was the shadow in right field that once had been Babe Ruth. Playing his final season in New York, the thirty-nine-year-old Babe hit just 22 home runs (including his 700th on July 13), drove in 84 runs, and batted .288—by his standards feeble numbers. During the winter all hands finally faced the inevitable and the Yankees gave their living legend his unconditional release, whereupon he was signed by the Boston Braves, who hoped he would be able to hype their attendance.

Ruth's final few years with the Yankees had been spent in a state of tension with McCarthy, whom the Babe was agitating to replace. The team, however, was more than satisfied with their manager, and in any event would not have hired Ruth, who was never to receive anywhere the offer to manage he so dearly coveted. The

albatross around the neck of Babe's managerial ambitions was manifest in the line uttered by Yankee general manager Ed Barrow: "If he can't even manage himself, how does he expect to manage twenty-five players?"

Being measured for the unenviable job of replacing Ruth in right field were George Selkirk and Dixie Walker, a couple of young, left-handed hitters. Selkirk would win the job and perform more than ably, while injuries would impede Walker, who years later would play for the Brooklyn Dodgers and become one of their most popular players.

Cleveland introduced a rookie first baseman with a booming bat in twenty-one-year-old Hal Trosky, who hit 35 home runs, drove in 142 runs (a rookie record that Ted Williams broke five years later), and batted .330. Trosky was one of five .300 hitters in the Indian lineup, along with outfielders Joe Vosmik (.341) and Earl Averill (.313), shortstop Bill Knickerbocker (.317), and second baseman Odell Hale (.302). Cleveland also had the league's fourth 20-game winner in right-hander Mel Harder (20–12).

Tom Yawkey had paid Connie Mack a lot of money to bring Lefty Grove to Boston and when baseball's greatest pitcher showed up at Fenway Park it was with a sore arm, the first that Lefty had ever suffered. The embarrassed Mr. Mack offered to do the honorable thing and return Yawkey's money, but the Boston millionaire graciously refused and instead watched Grove labor through an 8–8 season.

Sinking as slowly and surely as the evening sun, Connie Mack's A's were now in fifth place, despite some considerable punch at home plate. (They would not in fact even see fifth place again until 1944.) Jimmie Foxx continued making heavy contact, finishing second in home runs to Gehrig with 44, driving in 130

1·9·3·4

runs, and batting .334. (White Sox first baseman Zeke Bonura recalled in later years, "In 1934 I hit 27 home runs, had 110 RBIs, and batted .302, but with Gehrig, Foxx, Greenberg, and Trosky around, nobody even knew I was in the league.") Outfielder Bob Johnson hit 34 homers for the A's while ·batting .307, Doc Cramer rang up a .311 mark, and third baseman Pinky Higgins finished at .330; but while the A's could scare you with their hitting, the pitching staff's 5.01 ERA handed back more than their hitters gave them. Meanwhile, Connie was continuing the breakup of his 1929–31 pennant winners, this time selling George Earnshaw to the White Sox. Of the team that had terrorized the league just a few years before, only Foxx remained as a regular.

Washington's drop from the heights was precipitous—from first place to seventh in one year, despite four .300 hitters, including Heinie Manush at .349. Pitching woes crippled Joe Cronin's defending champions, with Earl Whitehill going from 22–8 to 14–11 and 1933's 24-game winner Alvin Crowder slogging along with a 4–10 record before being waived to Detroit in early August, where he won five of six.

Gehrig, remembered today both for his spectacular slugging and his bad luck, had a touch of each on June 30. On that day Lou whacked three triples against the Senators in 4½ innings, only to see the game washed out by rain before it was official.

Another tough-luck outing was experienced by the St. Louis Browns' right-hander Bobo Newsom. Witty, boastful, idiosyncratic, the hard-throwing Bobo was in some ways the American League's version of Dizzy Dean, though without Dean's infectious charm. On September 16, Bobo no-hit the Red Sox for nine innings, found himself in a 1–1 tie, and then lost it on a couple of walks and a hit in the tenth.

When it came around to World Series time, the effervescent Dizzy Dean announced that "Me 'n Paul are going to win two apiece." And this is just what they did, Dizzy winning Games 1 and 7 (he was beaten in Game 5) and Paul, always quietly amused by big brother's pronouncements, taking Games 3 and 6. But before it was over, one of the most tumultuous scenes in World Series history was played out.

The furor erupted in the seventh game—always a highly charged occasion to begin with. The Cardinals had torn open the game—played in Detroit—with a seven-run third inning, and Dizzy was pitching superbly. In the top of the sixth inning, the Cardinals scored twice more, one of the runs coming in on a Medwick triple. Joe's slide into third was deemed overly aggressive by Marv Owen and a near-altercation took place between Joe and the Tiger third baseman. The incident triggered the pent-up frustrations of the Detroit crowd, and when Medwick tried to take his left-field position in the bottom of the inning, he found himself being showered with various ripe edibles and other debris.

"I don't know where they were getting all the stuff from," Charlie Gehringer said. "It was almost as if somebody was backing up produce trucks at the gates and making deliveries."

After a 20-minute delay, during which the crowd remained unrelenting in its bombardment, Commissioner Landis ordered Medwick removed from the game, for the sake of decorum as well as Joe's safety. When the field was cleared and the crowd finally quieted, Dean completed an 11–0 blanking of the Tigers to give the Cardinals the world championship.

Dizzy Dean.

Born Jay Hanna Dean on January 16, 1911, in poverty-stricken Lucas, Arkansas, Dizzy Dean became in the early 1930s a symbol of joy, laughter, and hope when all seemed hopeless during the gloom of the Depression.

Dizzy spent just two years in the Cardinal farm system—for those days an unusually brief apprenticeship—before joining the big team in 1932, just twenty-one years old. It did not take long before the combination of talent and personality made him more than just a baseball celebrity. "Fresh as the morning dew," he charmed the press with his wisecracks and with a self-confidence that soon became boasting, normally an offensive quality, but in Dean laced with a beguiling innocence. According to Dizzy, "If you say you're going to do it, and then go out and do it, it ain't braggin'."

Ruth was fading, DiMaggio and Feller had not yet arrived, and so for several years in the mid-'30s Dean was baseball's number one draw, a national personality (and that magical nickname didn't hurt, either).

"You didn't have to know a thing about baseball," Hallahan said, "but you damned well heard of two guys—Babe Ruth and Dizzy Dean."

Along with everything else, Dean could be controversial, too—he argued with umpires, teammates, his manager, the league president. He skipped exhibition games during the season, was fined, suspended, cut up his uniform with a pair of scissors, insulted his employers, sulked, apologized, and always returned to cheers and adulation.

During the 1934 World Series he was a pinch runner and while trying to break up a double play was hit square in the head with the relay, was carried off the field, taken to the hospital, and returned with the imperishable quote, "They X-rayed my head and didn't find anything."

He won 30 in 1934, 28 the next year, 24 a year later, and was on the high road to another prosperous season when a foot injury in the 1937 All-Star Game spelled a sudden end to his career. His lifetime record is a superb 150–83.

But Dizzy Dean had become too deeply woven into the national fabric to disappear from public view. He re-emerged in the 1940s as a baseball announcer and with his zesty personality and colorful locutions charmed another genertion. (Players "slud" into bases, batters stood "confidentially" at the plate, etc.) Some of it was pure Dean, some probably a bit of calculated hokum—he always had natural show business instincts. Dizzy behind the microphone was a second career and a second legend.

Dean died on July 17, 1974, at the age of sixty-three.

Dizzy Dean.

Paul Dean.

Cardinals manager and second baseman Frank Frisch.
The 16-year veteran batted .305 as he led his club to the
1934 National League pennant.

Cardinal first baseman Rip Collins. A .333 hitter in 1934,
he drove in 128 runs and tied Mel Ott for the home-run
lead.

Joe Medwick. He drove in 106 runs in 1934 and led the league in triples with 18.

Cardinal catcher Spud Davis.

Pepper Martin doing the Gashouse Go-Out. The third baseman is Pittsburgh's Pie Traynor. The action is taking place at St. Louis's Sportsman's Park.

Hal Schumacher, a 23-game winner for the 1934 Giants.

Brooklyn Dodger manager Casey Stengel.

Mel Ott, the National League's home-run and RBI leader in 1934.

Mickey Cochrane, catcher and manager of the pennant-winning 1934 Detroit Tigers.

Detroit's young first baseman Hank Greenberg, who began showing his muscle in 1934 with 26 home runs, 139 RBIs, a .339 batting average, and a league-leading 63 doubles.

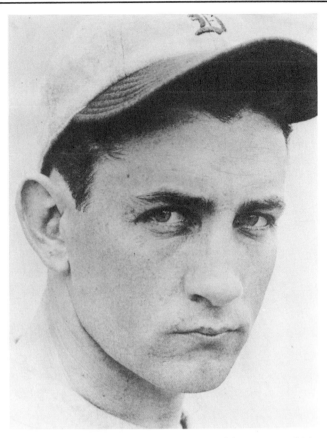

Charlie Gehringer. The greatest second baseman of his era, the Tiger star batted .356 in 1934, had 50 doubles, 127 RBIs, and led the league with 214 hits.

Tiger outfielder Pete Fox.

New York Giant catcher Gus Mancuso.

Detroit's Goose Goslin.

The Yankees' Lefty Gomez, who had his greatest year in 1934 with a 26–5 record.

Paul Waner, the National League batting champion in 1934.

Giant right-hander Roy Parmelee. His powerful physique earned him the nickname "Tarzan."

Former Yankee ace Waite Hoyt was 15–6 for the Pirates in 1934.

Cubs third baseman Stanley Hack.

Babe Ruth in 1934, his final year as a Yankee.

At bat for the Yankees, Number 4, Lou Gehrig.

Brooklyn first baseman Sam Leslie, a .332 hitter in 1934.

Brooklyn second baseman Lonny Frey.

Dodger right-hander Johnny Babich.

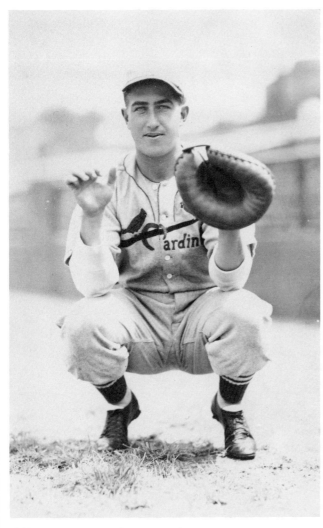

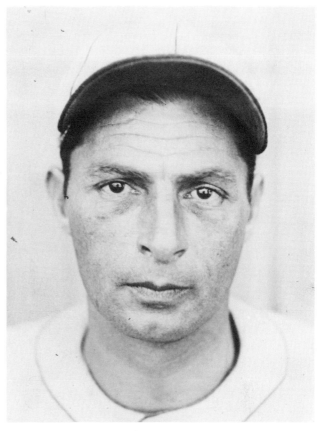

Ernie Orsatti, a .300-hitting outfielder for the Cardinals in 1934.

Bill DeLancey, the Cardinals' fine young catcher whose career was aborted by illness. Sharing the job with Spud Davis in 1934, DeLancey batted .316.

Cardinal shortstop Leo Durocher.   Schoolboy Rowe pausing for a dugout refresher.

The Dean brothers, Paul *(left)* and Dizzy.

Tiger third baseman Marv Owen, a .317 hitter in 1934.

Former Athletics ace George Earnshaw, who topped the White Sox staff with a 14–11 record in 1934.

Right-hander Tex Carleton, who was 16–11 for the Cardinals in 1934.

Outfielder Jo-Jo White, a .313 hitter for the 1934 Tiger pennant winners.

Paul Dean *(right)* covering first base and beating Brooklyn's Lonny Frey to the bag. This was the day Dean pitched his no-hitter.

Cincinnati outfielder Adam Comorosky.

Eldon Auker, who was 15–7 for the Tigers in 1934.

Detroit's Tommy Bridges, who opponents said had the best curve ball in the American League. Tommy was 22–11 in 1934.

Outfielder Ethan Allen, who played for six different teams in the 1930s. In 1934 he was with the Phillies, batting .330 and leading the league in doubles with 42.

Veteran shortstop Mark Koenig, who was with the Reds in 1934.

Right-hander Monte Pearson, who was 18–13 for the Indians in 1934.

It's August 25 and Schoolboy Rowe is in the midst of winning his record-tying 16th straight game. The game is being played at Griffith Stadium in Washington. The batter is Cecil Travis.

Cleveland's Mel Harder. He was 20–12 in 1934.

Fred Marberry. The former Washington star was 15–5 for the Tigers in 1934.

Philadelphia Phillies infielder Lou Chiozza.

Washington's Buddy Myer.

Philadelphia Athletics pitcher Johnny Marcum. He led the A's staff in 1934 with 14 wins.

Curt Davis. The tall right-hander was 19–17 for the Phillies in 1934.

Baseball's most traveled player, Bobo Newsom. Constantly traded, he played for six teams in the 1930s and nine overall during his 20-year career. In 1934 he was with the Browns, posting a 16–20 record.

Cleveland's slugging rookie first baseman Hal Trosky, who broke in with 35 home runs, 142 RBIs, and a .330 batting average.

Pepper Martin diving back to first on an attempted pickoff during the 1934 World Series. Hank Greenberg is the first baseman.

Action in Game 2 of the 1934 World Series. The Cardinals' Ernie Orsatti slides safely into third on a triple. Marv Owen is the Tiger third baseman and Number 5 is Hank Greenberg.

Starting pitchers for Game 4 of the 1934 World Series: Eldon Auker (left) and Tex Carleton.

Pinch runner Dizzy Dean has just been skulled by Detroit shortstop Billy Rogell's relay to first base in Game 4 of the 1934 World Series. Tiger second baseman Charlie Gehringer is at the right.

Dizzy Dean on the ground after being hit in the head. Kneeling over him is skipper Frankie Frisch.

Pepper Martin at work in the 1934 World Series. The catcher is Mickey Cochrane.

Charlie Gehringer.

1·9·3·5

Dizzy Dean had been spectacular in 1934, and he was almost as good in 1935, racking up a 28–12 record, and with brother Paul again winning 19, the Deans nearly matched their combined 49 victories of the year before. Nevertheless, the Cardinals were unable to repeat; the National League pennant winners in 1935 were Charlie Grimm's Chicago Cubs, by four games over the Gashouse Gang.

In winning, the Cubs were maintaining a curious three-year pattern, having previously won in 1929 and 1932. For much of the National League summer, however, it was a battle between the Cardinals and the Giants, with the Cubs hovering in third place. The Giants held the top position for virtually the entire season, until late August, when the Cardinals moved them aside. But then, in early September, the Cubs suddenly became, quite literally, unbeatable.

Baseball is a game that prides itself upon checks and balances, upon some arcane "law of averages" that prevents a man from hitting safely every time up, or a pitcher from winning every game, or teams—no matter how great or how inept—from winning or losing every game. But then in September 1935 that seemingly imperative law appeared to have been repealed, as the Cubs went on a 21-game winning streak. How did one account for this abrupt sundering of the game's cherished verities?

"Maybe it's the power of positive thinking," said Cubs second baseman Billy Herman, who thought quite positively that year with a .341 batting average, with 227 hits, including 57 doubles. "All of a sudden we got the notion that we couldn't lose; there was no way we

could lose. We came to the ball park every day, put on our uniforms and went out expecting to win. There were no pep talks, not a hell of a lot of backslapping; just this confidence that kept growing every day."

Phil Cavaretta, the club's eighteen-year-old rookie first baseman, remembered it this way: "You ever go 75 miles an hour on the highway while everyone else is doing 50? Well, that's how we felt."

The first 18 wins were scored at home, 4 games each from the visiting Eastern teams—Philadelphia, Boston, Brooklyn, and New York—and then two more from Pittsburgh. On September 25 the Cubs went to St. Louis for a five-game showdown series. Cavaretta's home run gave the Cubs a 1–0 win in the first game and a tie for the pennant, and then Grimm's team clinched it the next day when they beat Dizzy Dean 6–2. The 21st straight win came the day after that, and then the streak ended. It remains the second longest winning streak in major-league history, bettered only by the Giants' 26-game marathon in 1916.

In addition to Herman, the Cubs had another high-average man in catcher Gabby Hartnett (.344), the League's Most Valuable Player, while outfielders Frank Demaree (.325) and Augie Galan (.314) and third baseman Stan Hack (.311) also contributed solid seasons, helping the Cubs to a league-leading .288 team batting average. Ex-Phillies superstar Chuck Klein batted .293 and led the club in home runs with 21. Galan established a record by playing in 154 games and not once grounding into a double play.

Right-handers Bill Lee (20–6) and Lon Warneke (20–13) and lefty Larry French (17–10)

1·9·3·5

were at the top of a good starting rotation, followed by Charlie Root, Tex Carleton, and lefty Roy Henshaw.

In addition to Dizzy Dean, the dethroned Gashouse Gang received a handsome season from Joe Medwick, who batted .353 and drove in 126 runs, while first baseman Rip Collins batted .313 and had 122 RBIs.

Giants skipper Bill Terry batted .341 and the club also got .300 seasons from third baseman Travis Jackson and outfielders Mel Ott and Hank Leiber. Carl Hubbell, in the midst of his years of mastery, was 23–12 for the third-place Giants, and Hal Schumacher was 19–9. The team was hurt by Freddie Fitzsimmons's sore arm, which limited the knuckle baller to a 4–8 record; when good, however, he was very good—all four of Fitz's victories were shutouts.

Pittsburgh's Arky Vaughan ran away with the batting crown, the soft-spoken shortstop cracking the ball at a rarefied .385 clip, the highest mark ever by a National League shortstop, and more than half a century later no National Leaguer had bettered it. Arky's teammate, right-hander Cy Blanton, who was 18–13, was the ERA leader with a 2.58 ledger. In addition to Vaughan's smoking bat, the Pirates also had an all-.300-hitting outfield in Paul and Lloyd Waner and Woody Jensen.

After four straight years in last place, the Cincinnati Reds moved up to sixth, thanks primarily to a 22–13 year from Paul Derringer and catcher Ernie Lombardi's .343 batting average.

Last place belonged solidly to the Boston Braves, who sleepwalked to a 38–115 record (which left them 61½ games out of first place and 26 out of seventh). The Boston loss total was the National League record for the 154-game schedule. Nevertheless, the club did have a source of pride in Wally Berger, whose 34 home runs and 130 runs batted in led the league in each of these power categories. Wally was the only Boston Brave ever to lead in RBIs.

There were two high-interest stories in the National League in 1935, one awash with sentiment, the other an array of bright lights illuminating the way to the future.

The first story involved the man who is still the embodiment of baseball and its power to enchant. The Braves had signed Babe Ruth, hoping that his magic, though weighted with years, would help spin a few turnstiles. But the slow, fat, one-time Hercules of the diamond could no longer run, nor were his still poetically pure haymaker swings able to make consistent contact. Ruth retired on June 2, after 28 games, 72 at bats, just 13 hits, and a .181 batting average. Six of those hits had been home runs, with three of them coming on May 25 at Pittsburgh's spacious Forbes Field. This final, muscular display at twilight remains the coda of the Ruth legend, virtually his farewell to the game he had once upon a time made over into his own image and that he had come to personify and dominate.

"It was like watching a monument beginning to shake and crack," the Cubs' Fred Lindstrom said of the struggling Ruth. "You were waiting for it to topple. You know, when I think back on it, it was an awful thing to see."

The other story, almost simultaneous with the departure of Ruth, occurred on May 24 (a day before the Babe dispatched home runs number 712, 713, and 714), when Cincinnati's Crosley Field was the scene of major-league baseball's first night game. Cincinnati general manager Larry MacPhail had to use all of his considerable powers of persuasion to con-

1·9·3·5

vince the ever-conservative hierarchy of base-ball that night ball was the way of the future. As if to humor MacPhail, the league gave permission for the Reds to play seven night games that season. And so on the night of May 24, responding to the push of a button in the White House by President Franklin D. Roosevelt, 632 lamps at Crosley Field blazed to life and swept back the Ohio night. That first night game saw Derringer beat the Phillies, 2–1. (Within 13 years, every major-league team except the Cubs had installed lights.)

In the All-Star Game, the American League made it three wins in three games, defeating the Nationals by a score of 4–1. Jimmie Foxx drove in three runs with a two-run homer and a single.

About Washington owner Clark Griffith, a man who left pressure marks on every dollar he touched, it was said he would sell his own mother if the price was right. Well, it wasn't his mother, but in October 1934 the price had been right and Griff had put a member of the family on the block—his manager, shortstop, and son-in-law Joe Cronin. The price was $250,000, a truckful of money in those years. The purchaser was Red Sox owner Tom Yawkey, hell-bent on delivering a winner to Boston.

Yawkey installed Cronin at shortstop and hired the lantern-jawed San Francisco Irishman as manager, and waited for things to happen. What happened was the Sox won two more games than they did in 1934 (when they finished fourth), despite a 25–14 year from Wes Ferrell and a 20–12 comeback by Lefty Grove. Cronin batted .295 and led the team with 95 runs batted in, as the Red Sox again finished fourth. In addition to winning 25 games, Ferrell (who was caught this year by his brother Rick)

batted .347 and tied George Uhle's record for pitchers with 52 hits.

The pennant winners, for the second year in a row, were the Tigers. Mickey Cochrane's club took over first place from the Yankees in July and were never out of it again, finishing three ahead of Joe McCarthy's team, though Detroit was seven ahead when they clinched.

Cochrane's staff once again featured Tommy Bridges (21–10) and Schoolboy Rowe (19–13), plus Eldon Auker (18–7) and Alvin Crowder, who turned in his last winning season (16–10).

Getting better and better, Detroit first base-man Hank Greenberg batted .328 and led the league with a whopping 170 runs batted in and tied Jimmie Foxx for the home-run lead with 36. To Big Henry, the RBI was a tastier dish than the home run.

"To me," Greenberg said, "that was the biggest thrill, driving in a run."

"You could see Hank really bearing down out there with men on base," teammate Charlie Gehringer said. "He was always an intense hitter, but with men on base his concentration was really fierce." When Gehringer, batting ahead of Greenberg in the lineup, came to the plate with a man on first, the injunction from behind him was always, "Get him over to third, just get him over to third."

Along with Greenberg (the league's Most Valuable Player that year) and Gehringer, who batted .330, the Tigers mounted a well-balanced attack that included .300 hitters Cochrane and outfielders Pete Fox and Gerald Walker, helping the club to a .290 batting average, which was the best in a hard-hitting league that compiled an overall mark of .280.

"True, he hadn't been hitting all that well the

1·9·3·5

past year or two; all the same, they still weren't the same team without him. They didn't scare you as much."

The speaker was White Sox right-hander Ted Lyons, the "he" Ted was referring to was Babe Ruth and the "they" the New York Yankees. Playing without their great slugger for the first time in 15 years, the big team in the Bronx, though finishing second, did indeed seem to have a few front teeth missing. The Yankees' 104 home runs constituted the club's lowest total since 1924 and their 818 runs the lowest since 1925.

Lou Gehrig hit 30 homers, drove in 119 runs, and batted .329. (Underlining the dominance of Hank Greenberg this year was the fact that Gehrig's 119 RBIs were second to Big Henry's 170, a tremendous spread.) George Selkirk, Ruth's successor in right field, turned in a decent year under difficult circumstances, batting .312 and knocking in 94 runs, but hitting just 11 home runs, much to the chagrin of the right-field cheerleaders, who sorely missed their Babe.

"The fans made it very rough on George that year," McCarthy said. "Not only was he taking Ruth's place—if you can imagine anybody doing that—but the club had even assigned him Babe's Number 3. There was an awful lot of pressure on George, and I'd say he did just fine; but to a certain segment of the fans, nothing he did could be right and they booed him all season long. But he kept right at it and in a year or two they liked him just fine."

The Yankees had the best earned-run average in the league, 3.60, to Detroit's 3.82, but lacked the Tigers' big winners. Red Ruffing led the staff with a 16–11 record, but the biggest single factor for the New Yorkers' not winning in 1935 was the turn-around year suffered by

Lefty Gomez, who went from the luxurious heights of a 26–5 season in 1934 to a mediocre 12–15 in 1935.

Third-place Cleveland received a year of blistering hitting from Joe Vosmik, a home-grown product who was very popular with the Indian fans (which didn't stop the club from trading him a year later). Vosmik batted .348 and led the league in hits (216), doubles (47), and triples (20). Joe barely lost the batting crown during the season's waning at bats to Washington's Buddy Myer, who put together his finest year with a .349 average and 215 hits.

"He was a tough kid, that Myer," Ossie Bluege said of his Washington teammate. "Like a rock at second base. They'd come in with spikes flying and he never gave an inch, and if you didn't look out you might find yourself with a good kick in the ribs, and if you didn't like it, Buddy was right there to accommodate you."

In addition to Myer, the sixth-place Senators had four other .300 hitters in the lineup: third baseman Cecil Travis (.318), outfielders Johnny Stone (.315) and Jake Powell (.312), and catcher Cliff Bolton (.304). This was fairly typical of Washington hitting for the rest of the decade, but shoddy pitching always kept them tethered far from contention.

Some lusty hitting came from last place as well, where the Athletics batted .279 and led the league with 112 home runs, thanks primarily to Jimmie Foxx (36), Bob Johnson (28), and Pinky Higgins (23). Connie Mack also had Doc Cramer swinging a .332 bat and rookie Wally Moses breaking in with a .325 season, but the pitching staff's 5.12 ERA went a long way in nullifying much of that handsome hitting.

The seventh-place St. Louis Browns, seldom one of baseball's more riveting attractions, saw their attendance for 1935 sink to embarrassing

1·9·3·5

depths—record-low depths, in fact: 80,922, which is less than the single-day high of 84,587 that the Yankees and Indians drew for a doubleheader in Cleveland in 1954.

"It was a combination of things," Browns first baseman Jack Burns said. "The Depression, of course, was a factor. And St. Louis was a Cardinal town, same as Boston was a Red Sox town, and the Cardinals were a hot club in those years, what with Dean and Medwick and that bunch. And another thing that hurt was the Babe was gone. Don't kid yourself, when he came to town there were always a lot more people in the park, even when he was slowing down."

If Ruth's absence was felt around the league, it surely manifested itself most tellingly at home, where Yankee attendance dropped by over 200,000. The ever-resourceful Yankees, however, had another glittering draw waiting in the wings—they had purchased for 1936 delivery the contract of the minor leagues' most celebrated ballplayer, center fielder Joe DiMaggio of the San Francisco Seals.

In addition to Bridges, Ferrell, and Grove, Cleveland's Mel Harder (22–11) was also a "charmed-circle" winner. There was one no-hitter in the league this year, delivered by Chicago's Vern Kennedy, who stopped the Indians on August 31, 5–0.

After four visits to the World Series, the Detroit Tigers finally won one, upending the Cubs in six games to send the confetti flying and the horns blaring in Detroit. Cochrane's team won it in dramatic style, too. Going into the bottom of the ninth inning of Game 6 at Detroit, the clubs were locked in a 3–3 tie. With Cochrane on second base, Goose Goslin looped a single into short right-center to bring home the winning run, the world championship run.

"What a helpless feeling that was," Cubs second baseman Billy Herman said. "I was chasing it and so were the right and center fielders, and I knew nobody was going to get it. I can still hear that ball plopping onto the grass and then the Detroit crowd going crazy. Whenever I hear people say that baseball is fun, I always say, 'Yeah, sometimes.' "

Charlie Gehringer.

Charlie Gehringer

"We always took him absolutely for granted," Charlie Gehringer's Detroit teammate Hank Greenberg said of Gehringer. "We always expected him to be near-perfect, and he seldom disappointed."

Gehringer was born in Fowlerville, Michigan, on May 11, 1903. A friend brought him to Detroit for a tryout in 1924. The Tigers were then being managed by Ty Cobb, still an active player, and the team included such high-average hitters as Harry Heilmann and Heinie Manush. As Gehringer recalled it years later, the regulars "didn't like the idea of me getting in with them. But it was by Cobb's orders."

So the youngster stepped into the batting cage and began hitting. Cobb leaned on the rail of the cage and watched, and watched.

What happened after that, Gehringer said, "really amazed me. Cobb left the field and in full uniform, spikes and all, went up to Mr. Navin's office—he owned the ball club—and told Mr. Navin to come down to the field and watch me."

After two years in the minors, Gehringer took over second base for the Tigers in 1926 and made it his own until 1941, his last full season. He retired in 1942 with a lifetime average of .320.

Gehringer was a regular for 16 years, during which he batted over .300 13 times, collecting over 200 hits seven times, including five years in succession. In 8,860 official at bats he struck out just 372 times, a remarkable ratio made even more remarkable by an idiosyncracy he brought with him to the plate nearly every time—a reluctance to swing until he had a strike or two on him.

"I thought I was a better hitter with a strike or two on me," he said. "Too many times you go up there with the attitude of 'Well, this is the first pitch, I'll take a swing at it.' You're apt to be a bit careless, try to go for distance, and the next thing you know you've popped up. But with one strike or two strikes, you're not going to be careless. You really knuckle down. You're going to get a good pitch, and you're going to hit it."

Contact hitter though he was, Charlie was in double figures in home runs 11 times, with a high of 20 in 1938. Doubles were his specialty; seven times he had over 40, once 50, and once 60. He drove in over 100 runs seven times.

In the field he was smooth and graceful, playing second base with the same effortless grace that DiMaggio brought to center field, leading American League second basemen in fielding eight times.

Of the quietly efficient Gehringer, Lefty Gomez said, "You wind him up in the spring, turn him loose, he hits .330 or .340, and you shut him off at the end of the season."

Gabby Hartnett, catcher for the Chicago Cub pennant winners in 1935. Gabby batted a ripe .344.

Larry French, left-handed ace of the 1935 Cubs. He was 17–10.

Bill Lee. The big Cubs right-hander was 20–6 in 1935.

Detroit outfielder Gerald Walker.

Cubs pitcher Charlie Root, who was 15–8 in 1935.

Frank Demaree. The Cubs outfielder batted .325 in 1935.

Five infielders on the 1934 pennant-winning Chicago Cubs. *Left to right:* Woody English, Billy Herman, Charlie Grimm, Stanley Hack, and Billy Jurges.

Detroit Tigers manager Mickey Cochrane *(left)* and Eldon Auker.   Detroit shortstop Billy Rogell.

Dizzy Dean, a 28-game winner in 1935.

It looks like Schoolboy Rowe is going to fire that ball straight up. Rowe was 19–13 in 1935.

Tommy Bridges, who was 21–10 for the pennant-winning
Tigers in 1935.

Cardinal left-hander Bill Walker.

Goose Goslin.

Big Hank Greenberg, who drove in 170 runs in 1935.

Right-hander Alvin Crowder, whose 16 wins helped the Tigers to the pennant.

Giants outfielder Hank Leiber. He batted .331 and drove in 107 runs in 1935.

Yankee right-hander Johnny Broaca, who was 15–7 in 1935.

Washington's Buddy Myer, the American League's leading hitter in 1935.

The Giants' Hughie Critz raising the dust at home plate in the Polo Grounds. The catcher is Spud Davis.

At the age of eighteen, Phil Cavaretta was the regular first baseman for the 1935 pennant-winning Chicago Cubs.

Pittsburgh's Arky Vaughan, the National League's batting champion in 1935 with a snow-capped .385 average.

The Cubs' Augie Galan, who batted .314 in 1935 and led the league in stolen bases with 22.

George Selkirk had the unenviable task of replacing Babe Ruth in right field in Yankee Stadium. Once the fans realized there could never be another Ruth, they came to appreciate the hustling, sharp-hitting Selkirk.

Dizzy Dean *(left)* and Lon Warneke.

White Sox manager Jimmy Dykes.

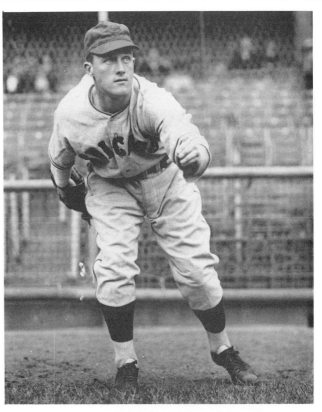

Cubs left-hander Roy Henshaw, who contributed a 13–5 record to the Chicago pennant effort.

Red Sox aces Wes Ferrell *(left)* and Lefty Grove. They won 45 games between them in 1935; nevertheless, each of these stalwarts is wearing his glove on the wrong hand.

Woody Jensen, an outfielder with a steady bat for the Pirates throughout the 1930s. In 1935 he had his best year—203 hits and .324 batting average.

Washington's Johnny Stone, a .315 hitter in 1935. Johnny was a .300 hitter six times in the 1930s, playing for the Tigers and Senators.

Cy Blanton. The Pittsburgh right-hander won 18 games in 1935 and led the National League in earned-run average. It was Blanton's first year in the big leagues and by far his best.

Joe Vosmik. The Cleveland outfielder had a big year in 1935, batting .348 and leading the league in doubles, triples, and hits.

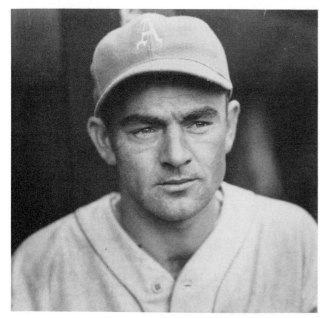

Wally Moses. The Athletics' rookie outfielder broke in with a .325 batting average. Wally was a .300 hitter his first seven years in the big leagues.

Cincinnati ace Paul Derringer, who was 22–13 for his sixth-place club in 1935.

Bobo Newsom. In 1935 he split his time between the Browns and Senators.

Cincinnati Reds second baseman Alex Kampouris.

Clydell (Slick) Castleman. The young Giant right-hander was 15–6 in 1935, his rookie year.

Former Athletics ace George Earnshaw working out with his son George, Jr. Earnshaw split the 1935 season between the White Sox and Brooklyn Dodgers.

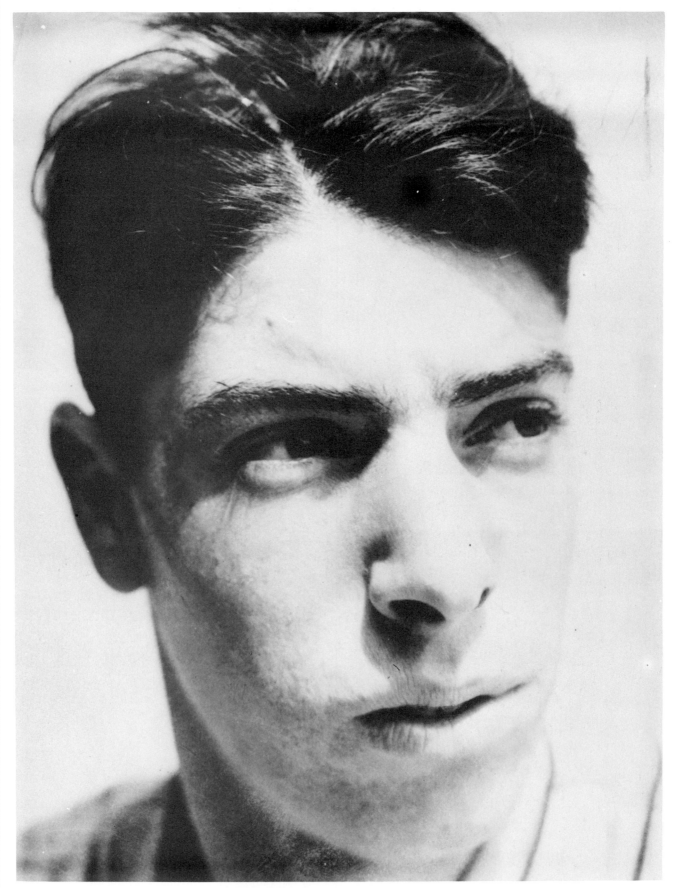

Meanwhile, out in the Pacific Coast League, San Francisco's twenty-year-old center fielder Joe DiMaggio (already purchased by the Yankees for 1936 delivery) was turning in a .398 batting average.

Detroit's Jo-Jo White swinging away in Game 3 of the 1935 World Series. The catcher is Gabby Hartnett.

Branch Rickey once described Dizzy Dean as "a man of mirth." Here is Dizzy *(left)* sharing some of it with Rickey *(center)* and Cardinals skipper Frankie Frisch.

A preseason gathering of some Boston notables. *Left to right:* Red Sox manager-shortstop Joe Cronin; the Braves' recent acquisition, Babe Ruth; and Braves manager Bill McKechnie. The forty-year-old Ruth played in just 28 games before retiring.

Carl Hubbell, who was 26–6 in 1936.

1·9·3·6

As it had been in 1921, 1922, 1923, and as it would be again many times in the 1940s and 1950s, New York was the baseball capital of the world in 1936 as both the Giants and Yankees won pennants.

At the end of July, Bill Terry's Giants were just a few games over .500, watching the Cardinals and Cubs arm wrestle at the top of the league. But then the Giants got caught up in a pair of very productive winning streaks. The first began on July 17, when Carl Hubbell won the first of 16 consecutive games, a string of success that carried right on through to the end of the season (and continued on with his first eight decisions in 1937). In winning his second MVP Award in four years, the screwballing southpaw put together his greatest season— 26–6, leading the league with a 2.31 ERA.

With Hubbell showing the way, the Giants in August launched a 15-game winning streak that shot them past the Cubs and enabled them to catch the Cardinals by the end of the month. The New Yorkers remained prosperous in September and wound up five games ahead of both the Cubs and Cardinals, who tied for second.

It was pretty much Hubbell on the mound for the Giants this year; the club's second-best winner was left-hander Al Smith, who was 14–13, as Hal Schumacher slumped to 11–13.

If Hubbell was the Giant pitching staff in 1936, then Mel Ott was the club's offensive attack. Now twenty-seven years old, the one-time "Master Melvin" (he came to the big leagues at the age of seventeen) hit 33 home runs to lead the league (no other Giant hit more than 9) and drove in 135 runs (no other Giant drove in more than 67), while batting .328. Outfielder Jo-Jo Moore, one of the team's steadier hitters in the 1930s, batted .316 and catcher Gus Mancuso, .301, while decent years were turned in by first baseman Sam Leslie, second baseman Burgess Whitehead, shortstop Dick Bartell, and outfielder Jimmy Ripple. Hobbled by bad knees, Terry put in his final year as an active player, getting into 79 games and batting .310.

The Cubs had enjoyed the view from first place until late in June, helped by a 15-game winning streak of their own earlier in the year.

"I wouldn't say absolutely," Cub third baseman Stan Hack recalled, "but that 15-game win streak might have started us thinking about the 21-game streak of the year before and made us just a bit overconfident, as if we could turn it on and off whenever we wanted. I thought we should have won in 1936, but it never quite happened."

The Cubs outhit the Giants by five points, .286 to .281, with several of their players enjoying highly successful seasons. Billy Herman, easily the best second baseman in the league, batted .334 and for the second year in a row had 57 doubles (only to finish second to Joe Medwick's National League record of 64); outfielder Frank Demaree batted .350 and catcher Gabby Hartnett, .307.

Bill Lee and left-hander Larry French topped the Cubs' staff with 18-win seasons.

Severely handicapping the Cardinals this year was the arm injury—all but career-ending—suffered by Paul Dean that reduced him to a 5–5 record. There was no one to pick up the slack and Dizzy couldn't do it by himself, though the self-proclaimed Great One did pitch to a 24–13 record, starting 34 games and

1·9·3·6

relieving in 17 others, as manager Frankie Frisch worked his always-willing ace to the limit. No other Cardinal pitcher won more than 11.

The gem-polishing operation that was the Cardinal farm system delivered another glittering package this year in first baseman Johnny Mize. The big, broad-shouldered, taciturn Mize, one of the most menacing-looking figures ever to stand at home plate, batted .329 in his rookie year, hitting 19 home runs and driving in 93 runs. The main St. Louis basher, however, remained Medwick, getting better every year as he hit .351 and led the league with 138 runs batted in.

After a couple of comparatively disappointing years with the Cubs, Chuck Klein found himself dealt back to the Phillies in late May. Two months later, on July 10, Klein enjoyed his greatest day in baseball when he slammed four home runs in a 10-inning game against the Pirates. Sweetening the occasion even more for Klein was the fact that the blasting wasn't done within the beckoning confines of Baker Bowl but rather in the considerably more spacious Forbes Field.

After having led in strikeouts his first four years in the league, Dizzy Dean found himself replaced at the top of the whiff brigade—and with plenty to spare—by Brooklyn's hard-throwing right-hander Van Lingle Mungo, 238 to 195. Mungo's total was the highest accumulation of strikeouts in the league since another Dodger right-hander, Dazzy Vance, had had 262 in 1924.

Decades later, his contemporaries still spoke in awe of Mungo's speed. How fast was the big South Carolinian? The question was put to Burleigh Grimes, who had pitched against Mungo and later managed him in Brooklyn.

"I didn't see that much of Walter Johnson," Grimes said, "but I saw plenty of Vance and Bob Feller and Mungo. I'd say if you dropped the three of them into a barrel and picked out one, you'd probably have as fast a right-hander as ever threw. When you're as fast as those boys were, then the differences between them is so slight as to be no difference at all."

Pitching for a seventh-place Dodger club (managed by Casey Stengel) and hampered by a league-high 118 walks, Mungo fast-balled himself to an 18–19 record.

Shutout honors were shared by seven National League pitchers this year with four apiece: Carl Hubbell; the Cubs' Larry French, Bill Lee, Lon Warneke, and Tex Carleton; the Pirates' Cy Blanton; and the Phillies' Bucky Walters. Walters, a light-hitting third baseman, had been converted to the mound the year before, posting a 9–9 record. In 1936 he was 11–21 for the last-place Phillies. Bucky had made the transition grudgingly, at the behest of manager Jimmie Wilson.

"I didn't like it at first," Bucky said. "I wanted to play third base."

"He had an incredibly live arm," Wilson said. "I used to watch his pegs fly across the infield and just marvel at how much he had on the ball. There were times the ball moved so much the first baseman had trouble handling it."

Wilson, a canny catcher for the Phillies and Cardinals in his younger days, knew exactly what he was doing. In a few years Walters—pitching for Cincinnati—would become the king of National League pitchers.

The National League finally won its first All-Star Game this year, 4–3. They did it by throwing Dean and Hubbell at the American Leaguers for the first six innings, building up a 4–0 lead that they just did hold on to.

1·9·3·6

Certain years in baseball history have become associated with players or teams or events: 1914 is the year of "The Miracle Braves"; 1927 is the year of the Yankees and Babe Ruth's 60 home runs; 1951, the year of Bobby Thomson's spectacularly dramatic home run; 1969, the year of the New York Mets. Well, 1936 was the year of the "Golden Rookies" in the American League. They were named DiMaggio and Feller, and they were young and not just instantly successful, but more: instantly glamorous and charismatic, each a rivetingly singular athlete, obviously come to mold new standards.

Joe DiMaggio was just twenty-one years old when he took command of center field in Yankee Stadium. Asked to patrol one of baseball's most spacious regions, he did it with such smooth and unerring judgment that some fans, watching the same play, could argue whether Joe had been playing unusually deep or fortuitously shallow, for how else could he have snatched from the air all ranges of line drives and fly balls with the exertion of so little effort? The secret was judgment—DiMaggio claimed that the instant a ball went into the air he knew within five feet where it would come down.

Only the New York Yankees could have had the audacity to hope for a replacement for Ruth, for a new titan to team with Gehrig, and maybe it was the very extravagance of the dream that made it happen.

But it was more than Gehrig that DiMaggio joined in the 1936 Yankee lineup; there were also the veteran Tony Lazzeri, still at second base, and Bill Dickey behind the plate, Red Rolfe at third, and George Selkirk and Jake Powell in the outfield. This lineup produced a .300 batting average, led by Dickey's .362, the highest ever recorded by a catcher. Gehrig—

the Most Valuable Player this year—batted .354, hit 49 home runs, and drove in 152 runs. Lou was one of a record five Yankees to drive in over 100 runs, the others being Lazzeri, Selkirk, Dickey, and the new man, DiMaggio. Joe broke in with a .323 average, 29 home runs, and 125 RBIs.

It was a free-hitting season in the American League, the collective .289 batting average being the league's highest of the decade. Accordingly, the Yankees' 1,065 runs established a major-league record that still stands, and their 182 home runs set a record for the time. The Yankee pitching staff had an earned-run average of 4.17—very high, but that year the lowest in the league. Joe McCarthy's big winners were Red Ruffing (20–12) and Monte Pearson (19–7). Pearson had been acquired from Cleveland in a deal for the tempestuous Johnny Allen (who was a 20-game winner for the Indians).

The Yankees, who averaged nearly 7 runs a game, had their season keynoted on May 24 when Lazzeri hit 2 grand slammers in one game and drove in 11 runs in a 25–2 Yankee massacre of the Athletics. Lazzeri still holds the American League single-game RBI record.

Joe McCarthy's club broke away fast and was never threatened or ever seriously pursued, winning 102 games and taking the pennant by 19½ games over second-place Detroit, who never really had a chance to make it three in a row. The Tigers lost their big slugger Hank Greenberg after 12 games to a broken wrist, and then in midseason their manager-catcher Mickey Cochrane suffered a mental breakdown and had to leave the team. It is doubtful, however, that even at full strength the Tigers would have been able to successfully challenge the Yankees.

1·9·3·6

Charlie Gehringer batted .354 and had 227 hits, including 60 doubles, fourth highest total in league history, and outfielders Gerald Walker, Al Simmons, and Goose Goslin were each comfortably over .300. The Tigers, who tied the Yankees with a .300 team batting average, had four men with over 100 runs batted in: Gehringer, Simmons, Goslin, and Marv Owen. Detroit's mound aces also had big seasons, with Tommy Bridges at 23–11 and Schoolboy Rowe at 19–10.

There were sumptuous batting averages all around the league this freewheeling season, but none better than the .388 raised by White Sox shortstop Luke Appling, a figure that eclipsed the .385 standard that Arky Vaughan had established for shortstops just the year before.

"Old aches and pains," White Sox manager Jimmy Dykes called Appling. "He'd come to the park walking like an old man, complaining of this, that, and the other thing. 'You look fine to me,' I'd tell him. 'Go out there and get three hits.' There was never anything wrong with him. Hypochrondiac he was."

Appling was known for his ability to foul off two-strike pitches that he didn't care to swing at and that were too close to take. And occasionally, against a hotheaded pitcher like Wes Ferrell, Luke would do it just for mischief.

"That S.O.B. once fouled off about twelve three-two pitches in a row on me," Ferrell said. "It was a hot day in Chicago, maybe 100 degrees, and he was trying to wear me out. I kept powderin' it in there and he just kept nicking them here and there. Having a good ol' time for himself. I finally walked him. Next time up he knew he was for it. I figured I'd get a strike on him and then put one under his chin. But the S.O.B. must have read my mind because he

swung at the first pitch and got out of there."

Cleveland's Earl Averill batted .378 and led with 232 hits, while his teammate Hal Trosky had a thunderous year with a .343 average, 42 home runs, and 162 RBIs.

"I got into a little trouble in Cleveland that year," McCarthy said. "I think it was in July or August. A couple of the Cleveland writers were saying what a great year Trosky was having. And he was—Hal was a fine hitter. But I said, 'Trosky is doing this year what Gehrig does every year.' They got on me for that."

In Boston, Tom Yawkey was still playing checkbook baseball. This time, for $135,000, he had bought Jimmie Foxx from the A's. Jimmie responded with a typical Jimmie Foxx year—.338 batting average, 41 home runs, 143 RBIs. Nevertheless, the Red Sox finished sixth, despite a 20–15 year from Ferrell and a 17–9 showing from Grove, who also led with a 2.81 ERA, exceedingly low for that season.

Chicago's Vern Kennedy turned in a 21–9 record, giving the league five 20-game winners; none of them, however, excited fans as much as a seventeen-year-old Cleveland right-hander who was just five and three.

Bob Feller captured the national imagination as few pitchers ever had, before or since. His youth and blinding speed made the boy a phenomenon. Signed by Cleveland scout Cy Slapnicka in 1935 for a bonus of one dollar, Feller was deemed too valuable to be entrusted to minor-league handling and spent the first half of the season traveling and working out with the Indians as a nonroster player.

During the All-Star break in July, the Indians had scheduled an exhibition game with the Cardinals. Cleveland decided to take this opportunity to put their youngster on the mound against some live major-league hitting.

1·9·3·6

The Iowa farmboy accepted the assignment with equanimity.

"No," Feller said. "I wasn't nervous. I was never nervous on a pitching mound."

No, not with that fast ball, which he buzzed at the Cardinals for three innings, fanning eight and making jittery wrecks of them all (the young Rapid Robert could be frighteningly wild). The story made headlines and the performance put Feller on the active roster. In his first big-league start, against the St. Louis Browns on August 23, young Bobby whiffed 15. On September 13, he struck out 17 Philadelphia Athletics, breaking Rube Waddell's American League record of 16 and tying Dizzy Dean's major-league mark.

"That's when people began to realize I was for real," Feller said.

He was almost beyond being real, with a fast ball that traveled close to 100 miles per hour and a big, fast, sharp-breaking curve that right-handed hitters said should have been declared illegal. It was one of the least hittable pitches in baseball history, to the extent that some managers flashed their weaker right-handed hitters the "take" sign on three-and-two against Feller, reasoning that they weren't going to hit it anyway and maybe it would be ball four.

Bobby began the creation of the Feller legend that summer, and then after the season went back to Van Meter, Iowa, studied hard, and graduated from high school.

The American League's sharp hitting all summer saddled the pitchers with a composite 5.04 ERA, highest in league history. Was the ball livelier in 1936? Different witnesses had different perspectives.

"It seemed the same to me," Charlie Gehringer said.

"It was definitely juiced up," Wes Ferrell said. (Despite winning 20 games, Wes gave up 330 hits in 301 innings, making his testimony somewhat suspect.)

Cleveland's cold-blooded Johnny Allen, who never had compunctions about knocking a man down (whether it was in a bar or at home plate), had his own opinion, and he gave it to pitcher Kirby Higbe when both were with Brooklyn in 1942.

"He told me," said Higbe, "that the ball was very lively in 1936. He knew it because once he hit some guy in the head with a pitch and the ball went on the fly into the box seats. I never knew if he was kidding or not. But anyway, that's the way Johnny Allen would measure things."

The Yankees began staking out the World Series as their own personal domain that year, taking the first of four consecutive world championships. McCarthy's men capsized the Giants in six games and in Game 4 did something the National League had been unable to do the last ten weeks of the season—they defeated Carl Hubbell.

Joe DiMaggio.

Joe DiMaggio

Joe DiMaggio is one of the few American athletes to transcend his sport and secure a place in the national consciousness. For DiMaggio, described as "the sleekest ship of state ever to play America's game," it was a combination of baseball skills, marriage to Marilyn Monroe, and an enduring personal mystique that elevated him to a unique place in the pantheon.

Son of an Italian immigrant fisherman, DiMaggio was born in Martinez, California, on November 25, 1914. After a spectacular several seasons playing for the San Francisco Seals in the Pacific Coast League (his achievements included a 61-game hitting streak and a .398 batting average), he joined the Yankees in 1936, so heralded that he was a star before he played a single big-league game.

He was manager Joe McCarthy's "perfect player."

"He could do everything that a player was called upon to do," McCarthy said, "and do it better than anybody else. He had perfect instincts, perfect judgment. I don't think I ever saw him make a mistake on a ball field. And," the manager added, "he was a nice fellow, too. Never made any trouble. Like Gehrig." (That "Like Gehrig" was as high an accolade as McCarthy could possibly give any ball player.)

"Joe played with tremendous intensity," Bob Feller said. "There weren't many batters you could *feel* concentrating up at the plate. Williams was one, of course, and Joe was another."

With his career interrupted for three years by military service in World War II, DiMaggio played for 13 years, batting over .300 in 11 of them. (In 10 of those 13 years the Yankees won pennants.) Nine times he drove in over 100 runs, including 167 in 1937 and 155 in 1948. He hit over 30 homers in a season seven times, leading the league twice.

In 1941, DiMaggio enthralled the nation for much of the summer with his 56-game hitting streak, one of the landmark achievements in the history of sports. The record itself is almost metaphoric, for it represents the DiMaggio phenomenon: consistency and superb response to pressure (no pressure in sports has quite the incremental force of a prolonged batting streak). The streak helped Joe earn one of his three Most Valuable Player Awards, the others coming in 1939 and 1947.

After a disappointing .263 season in 1951, the thirty-seven-year-old DiMaggio retired, taking with him a .325 lifetime average. He could have played another year or two, and the Yankees certainly wanted him to, but DiMaggio said, "I will not embarrass myself on a ball field."

The "Golden Rookies" of 1936: Joe DiMaggio *(left)* and Bob Feller.

Yankee catcher Bill Dickey, who in 1936 set an all-time record for catchers with his .362 batting average.

Lou Gehrig.

Joe 'DiMaggio.

Yankee third baseman Red Rolfe, who batted .319 for the 1936 American League pennant winners.

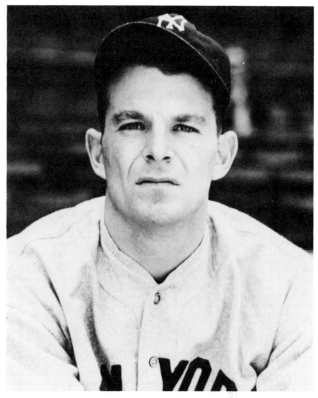

George Selkirk. He had 107 RBIs in 1936, one of five Yankees to knock in over 100 runs that year.

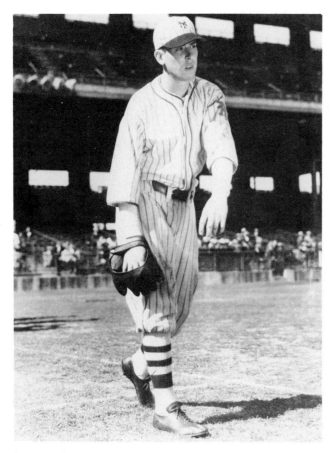

Giants left-hander Al Smith. He had a 14–13 record in 1936.

Mel Ott in his famous high-kicking batting posture. He was the National League home-run leader in 1936.

Shortstop Frank Crosetti (left) and second baseman Tony Lazzeri of the 1936 Yankees. Crosetti's .288 batting average that year was the highest of his 17-year career.

Giants shortstop Dick Bartell. His spirited style of play earned him the nickname "Rowdy Richard."

Jo-Jo Moore, who had 205 hits and batted .316 for the pennant-winning Giants in 1936.

Johnny Mize, the Cardinals' rookie first baseman who broke in with a .329 batting average.

Joe Medwick, who took the first of three straight RBI crowns in 1936 while setting a league record with 64 doubles.

Goose Goslin. The Tiger veteran had 125 RBIs in 1936, the 11th and final time he totaled 100 or more RBIs in a season.

Cardinal center fielder Terry Moore, who was considered to have no peer on defense.

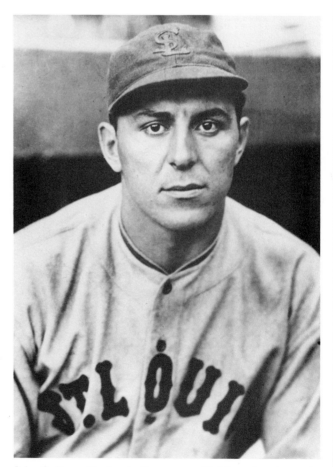

Jake Solters, St. Louis Browns outfielder who drove in 134 runs in 1936.

Beau Bell. The Browns outfielder had a big year in 1936, driving in 123 runs, collecting 212 hits, and batting .344. Bell did just as well in 1937, but quickly lost his touch thereafter.

After pitching for the Senators, White Sox, and Browns, Bump Hadley landed with the Yankees in 1936, just in time to start cashing World Series checks. He was 14–4 that year.

Browns manager Rogers Hornsby.

Detroit's Gerald Walker, who batted .353 in 1936.

Buddy Hassett, Brooklyn's line-drive-hitting rookie first baseman who broke in with a .310 batting average.

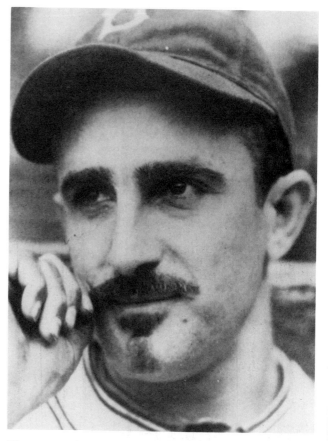

That mustache Dodger outfielder Frenchy Bordagaray is sporting caused quite a scandal when he turned up with it at Brooklyn's 1936 spring training camp. After being ordered to shave it off, the colorful Frenchy went on to bat .315 for the Brooks.

Brooklyn Dodger outfielder Johnny Cooney. Johnny played in the big leagues for 20 years and hit just two home runs—on successive days in 1939.

Dodger right-hander Max Butcher, a rookie in 1936. Max later had fair success pitching for the Pirates in the 1940s.

Brooklyn's Babe Phelps seems ready for just about anything up at home plate. The Dodger catcher got into 115
games in 1936 and batted a robust .367.

Giants outfielder Jimmy Ripple eyeing the ball he's just
hit. Jimmy batted .305 for the National League pennant
winners in 1936.

Yankee right-hander Monte Pearson, who had a fine
19–7 record for the 1936 pennant winners.

The Yankees' Red Ruffing, who launched four straight
20-game seasons with a 20–12 record in 1936.

New York Giants relief pitcher Dick Coffman.

Appearing mostly in relief for the Giants in 1936, right-hander Harry Gumbert posted an 11–3 record.

Giants first baseman Sam Leslie. Sam was reacquired from the Dodgers in 1936.

Carl Hubbell pitching to the Pirates' Al Todd at the Polo Grounds.

Pirate third baseman Bill Brubaker, who drove in 102 runs in 1936.

Claude Passeau, right-hander for the Philadelphia Phillies. He was 11–15 for the last-place Phillies in 1936.

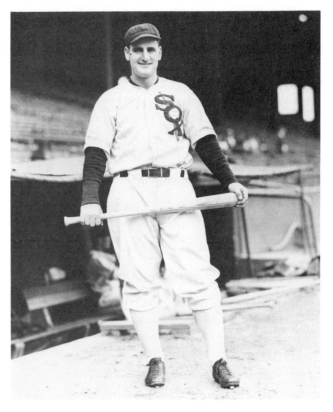

Zeke Bonura. The White Sox first baseman batted .330 in 1936 and drove in 138 runs.

St. Louis Browns right-hander Jack Knott. Jack managed nine wins in 1936 despite a horrendous 7.29 ERA.

Red Lucas, one of the great hitting pitchers of all time (lifetime average .281). In 1936 the right-hander was 15-4 for the Pirates. Red led the National League four times in pinch hits.

Schoolboy Rowe. He was 19–10 for the Tigers in 1936.

Goose Goslin showing his form.

Al Simmons, who played for Detroit in 1936. Al batted .327 and drove in 112 runs. It was his 12th and final 100-RBI season.

White Sox shortstop Luke Appling showing how easy it could be. In 1936 it was especially easy for Luke; he won the batting crown with a .388 average, highest ever for a shortstop.

They generated enough power to illuminate a city. Jimmie Foxx *(left)* and Lou Gehrig.

First baseman-outfielder Lou Finney of the Philadelphia Athletics. He batted .302 in 1936 and had 197 hits.

Cleveland's Earl Averill, who ripped the ball for a .378 average in 1936, leading the league with 232 hits.

White Sox right-hander Vern Kennedy had his best year in 1936, going 21–9.

Bob Feller.

Roy (Stormy Weather) Weatherly. The Cleveland outfielder batted .335 in 1936, his rookie year. He never hit that high again.

Young Mr. Feller showing his eight-year-old sister Marguerite how to throw that big curve.

Hal Trosky. His 162 RBIs led the league in 1936.

Cleveland infielder Odell Hale, whose nickname was "Bad News." Four times a .300 hitter in the 1930s, Bad News reached his peak with .316 in 1936.

Outfielder Bruce Campbell got into just 76 games for the Indians in 1936, but he batted .372. Bruce was hampered by illness.

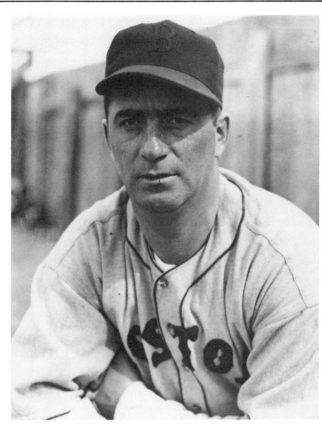

Red Sox catcher Moe Berg. Always a backup catcher, Moe was known as baseball's most erudite man. The line on him was he could speak eleven languages and not hit in any of them.

Braves second baseman Tony Cuccinello, who also played for the Reds and Dodgers in the 1930s. He batted .308 in 1936.

Celebrating their victory over the Giants in the 1936 World Series are four members of the world champion Yankees. *Left to right:* Bill Dickey, Johnny Murphy, Red Rolfe, and George Selkirk. The scene is Leon and Eddie's, a popular New York night spot of the time.

Out of baseball for the first time since 1914, the Babe seems to be taking it all in stride.

After getting his man at second, Yankee shortstop Frank Crosetti is firing on to first for the double play.

1·9·3·7

New York remained the center of the baseball universe in 1937 as both the Yankees and Giants repeated as pennant winners. For Giants manager Bill Terry, it was his third pennant in his fifth full year of running the club, and he was able to accomplish it despite the loss of one of the team's greatest assets—his own performance at first base; he retired as a player after the '36 season because of aching knees.

After trailing the Cubs throughout much of July and August, the Giants put on a spirited September drive that carried them past the Cubs and into first place, where they finished the season, three games ahead of Chicago.

The Giants still had one of baseball's primary assets in Carl Hubbell, who turned in his fifth consecutive (and last) season of 20 or more victories (22–8). This five-year run of sustained brilliance left the stamp of greatness upon the career of Carl Hubbell and created his candidacy for the Hall of Fame (which had been established in Cooperstown, New York, the year before). Hubbell began the season with 8 consecutive wins, giving him a string of 24 in a row, before being defeated by Brooklyn on May 30.

King Carl was abetted this year by another big-winning left-hander, rookie Cliff Melton, a twenty-five-year-old freshman who broke in with what proved to be his best major-league season, 20–9. Melton pitched another seven years in the bigs but never came close to repeating that rookie showing. According to one explanation, Melton, who idolized Hubbell, tried to emulate the master by developing a screwball, a most difficult delivery and acknowledged to be rough on the arm. Despite being warned that the pitch was not for him,

Melton persisted with it and damaged his arm just enough to remove the gloss of ever being a 20-game winner again.

Mel Ott was still the Giants' main belter, hitting 31 home runs (tying Joe Medwick for the lead) and batting in 95 runs. The club also got good seasons from shortstop Dick Bartell, second baseman Burgess Whitehead, catcher Harry Danning, and outfielders Jo-Jo Moore and Jimmy Ripple.

Charlie Grimm's second-place Cubs led the league with a .287 batting average, getting strong performances from veteran catcher Gabby Hartnett (.354), second baseman Billy Herman (.335), and outfielder Frank Demaree (.324). The Cubs, however, had traded one of their top pitchers, Lon Warneke, to the Cardinals for first baseman Rip Collins, who had a disappointing year, and right-hander Roy Parmelee, who was 7–8. Warneke went on to win 18 for the Cardinals.

"That trade hurt us," Hartnett said. "It probably cost us the pennant in '37."

Chicago's top winners were Tex Carleton and Larry French with 16 apiece.

Beginning in 1932, the Pittsburgh Pirate team batting averages read like this: .285, .285, .287, .285, .286, and in 1937 .285, giving the club a sturdy consistency. The Pirates, however, didn't hit many home runs and lacked a big winner on the mound. In 1937, Paul Waner batted .354; Lloyd Waner, .330; Arky Vaughan, .322; and catcher Al Todd, .307.

"You never saw so many singles in your life," Lloyd Waner said. "What we were missing was that big guy to come up every so often and clean off the bases with one swing."

The "big guy" was in St. Louis in 1937, his

1·9·3·7

name Joe Medwick. Joe turned in a bruising MVP, Triple Crown season that saw him lead in just about every available offensive category. In addition to his Triple Crown figures—.374 batting average, 31 home runs (tied with Ott), and 154 runs batted in—the Cardinals' testy, sullen mass of muscles topped the league in slugging (.641), total bases (406), hits (237), runs (111), and doubles (56). He probably led in stiffing waiters, too, for the rock-fisted Joe seems to have been tightfisted as well; for, as one teammate put it, "Joe thinks tipping is a city in China."

Right up there in most categories with Joe was teammate Johnny Mize. The big, powerful first baseman paced Joe to the batting title with a .364 average, hit 25 homers, 40 doubles, had 204 hits, and knocked in 113 runs.

The Boston Braves had an unusual pair of one-year wonders in rookie right-handers Lou Fette and Jim Turner, although the "rookie" designation should perhaps be footnoted: Lou was thirty years old and Jim thirty-three. Fette was 20–10 with five shutouts and Turner was 20–11 with five shutouts and the league's lowest ERA, 2.38, making him the first Braves pitcher ever to lead in that department. Giving these records an added luster was the fact that the Boston team batting average of .247 was the lowest in the league. Along with the Giants' Melton, this gave the league the rarity of three 20-game-winning rookies in the same year; but all three followed similar downhill courses after that season, none of them ever coming close to regaining the heights of initial conquest.

An old familiar American League face appeared in the National League this year when the Dodgers acquired Heinie Manush from the Red Sox. Playing for Burleigh Grimes's bumbling sixth-place 91-game losers, the veteran Manush's bat sprayed enough hits for a .333 average (three points over his lifetime mark).

"Heinie was our team in 1937," Grimes said. "There were times when I was tempted to list him second, fourth, and sixth in the lineup, but I didn't think I'd get by with it."

The American League won the All-Star Game by a score of 8–3, but that wasn't the big story. The big story of that game, in fact, wasn't realized until weeks after the event, when it developed into one of the saddest of all baseball stories.

In the bottom of the third inning Dizzy Dean, who had started for the National League, was hit on the foot by a scorching line drive off the bat of Cleveland's Earl Averill. The impact broke one of Dean's toes. Instead of waiting for the broken digit to fully heal, the impatient Dean was soon back on the mound. Why the Cardinals allowed this has never been satisfactorily explained. One theory holds that the club didn't want to lose their top draw for more than a few starts; another, that Dean insisted, which, if true, still places the onus on the club for allowing him.

In trying to compensate for the pain and discomfort he still felt, Dean altered his pitching motion, despite a stern warning from Boston manager Bill McKechnie, who saw the danger. The stubborn Dean would not listen, and a few weeks after the accident he injured his arm. All of a sudden, the famous fast ball was gone, and at the age of twenty-six Dizzy Dean was finished as a significant force and factor in baseball.

The following spring the Cardinals sold Dean to the Cubs for $185,000. The Cubs knew they were getting damaged goods; nevertheless, Dizzy's aura was still bright enough to

Bill Dickey. He helped the Yankees to a second straight pennant with 133 runs batted in and .332 batting average.

A dapper young Joe DiMaggio seems all set for summer in New York. For Joe it was a good summer—he led the league with 46 home runs and drove in 167 runs.

Nineteen thirty-seven was the final year in a Yankee uniform for veteran second baseman Tony Lazzeri, whose average dipped to .244 this year.

1·9·3·7

enchant them into wanting to possess him. In Chicago, the one-time speedballer tried to become a finesse pitcher, but with nothing to set up his slow curves, his effectiveness waned and one of baseball's all-time great careers crashed like the metaphoric meteor.

Whatever chance the Detroit Tigers might have had of unseating the Yankees at the top of the American League and reclaiming the title they had won in 1934 and 1935 ended early in the 1937 season. Schoolboy Rowe, one of their aces for the past three years, came up with a sore arm that kept him out of action for the better part of two years, and then there was the near-fatal injury to the club's catcher-manager Mickey Cochrane. Standing at home plate in Yankee Stadium on May 25, Cochrane lost a Bump Hadley fast ball in the white-shirted center field background and was struck flush in the head. The blow ended Cochrane's career and almost his life.

Without Rowe and Cochrane, the Tigers finished second, 13 games behind Joe McCarthy's steamrolling Yankees, who, while not quite as awesome as the year before, nevertheless again won 102 games. Where the Yankees had six .300 hitters among their regulars the year before, this time they had four, but three of them were extremely potent. For Lou Gehrig it was his final year of superproduction; the by-now monumental Yankee first baseman batted .351, hit 37 home runs, and drove in 159 runs. Sophomore Joe DiMaggio rang up a .346 average, hit 46 home runs, and knocked in 167 runs. Bill Dickey batted .332, had 29 homers and 133 RBIs. A very strong case could be made that these three belong on baseball's all-time all-star team, and here they were, playing at the same time, on the same team.

The rest of McCarthy's infield, Tony Lazzeri, Frank Crosetti, and Red Rolfe, each had subpar years (for the veteran Lazzeri, it was his final year with the Yankees), but outfielders Myril Hoag, George Selkirk, and rookie Tommy Henrich all hit extremely well.

Lefty Gomez was 21–11 for McCarthy and Red Ruffing 20–7, with Lefty the ERA leader with 2.33. The Yankees also received winning seasons from Hadley and Monte Pearson, as well as first-rate relief pitching from Johnny Murphy, who was 13–4.

The second-place Tigers saw their two great "G-Men," Greenberg and Gehringer, turn in outstanding seasons. Gehringer was the league's Most Valuable Player, leading with a .371 batting average, the best of his career. Greenberg accumulated a mammoth 183 RBI total, one under Gehrig's league record. In addition, the big twenty-six-year-old slugger batted .337 and hit 40 home runs.

Leading the league with a .292 team average, the Tigers had three more .300 hitters in outfielders Pete Fox and Gerald Walker and the power-hitting (35 homers) Rudy York, who replaced Cochrane behind the plate. The Tigers also tied a major-league record set by the 1929 Phillies when four of their players collected 200 or more hits—Gehringer, Greenberg, Fox, and Walker. This brand of hitting carried right-hander Roxie Lawson to an 18–7 record, despite an ERA of 5.27, highest on the team.

"I wouldn't say Roxie was lucky that year," the whimsical Gerald Walker said. "But I would say that he was always out there at the right time."

The tempestuous Johnny Allen gave the Cleveland Indians a nearly flawless season's work, running up a 15–1 record, with the loss coming on the final day of the season. Young

1·9·3·7

Bob Feller was 9–7 with 150 strikeouts in 149 innings, an impressive ratio in that era of fewer strikeouts. Bob's season was limited to 19 starts because of arm trouble, a condition that alarmed the Cleveland front office, for the eighteen-year-old was rapidly becoming baseball's number-one attraction.

"It was a soreness," Cleveland outfielder Earl Averill said of Feller's problem. "I don't think it was ever very serious, but the front-office people got a lot of gray hairs until it was healed."

The White Sox' genial first baseman Zeke Bonura, described by Paul Richards as "one of baseball's great conversation pieces," was fourth in batting with a .345 average. Zeke was noted for his sunny disposition, his strong hitting, and his immobility at first base, with two of these being wrapped up in one writer's observation that "Zeke never failed to wave at any grounder that came near him."

With the league batting .281, there was some gaudy hitting in every port, including a .344 average from Washington shortstop Cecil Travis, whose potentially Hall of Fame career was shattered by service in World War II. Some of the steadiest contact was made by the St. Louis Browns, whose .285 team average was two points better than the pennant-winning Yankees', but who finished last nevertheless, losing 108 games, thanks to an overly generous pitching staff that recorded an ERA of 6.00 and allowed 1770 hits, just 6 under the league record they had established the year before. The club had outfielder Beau Bell bat .340 and lead the league with 218 hits, outfielders Sammy West, Joe Vosmik, and Ethan Allen batted .328, .325, and .316, respectively, while third baseman Harlond Clift hit .306 and had 29 home runs.

In this year of well-nourished batting averages, the White Sox' Bill Dietrich managed a no-hitter, stopping the Browns on June 1, 8–0. It was only the fifth no-hitter pitched in the American League since 1926.

The World Series was a rather tame affair, the well-oiled Yankee machine punching out the Giants in five games. Gomez, who had beaten the Giants twice in 1936, did the same in 1937. Hubbell saved the Giants from the embarrassment of a sweep when he won Game 4 for his club.

"We almost swept them," McCarthy said. "But it was never a disgrace to lose to Carl Hubbell."

Joe Medwick.

When the St. Louis Cardinals won the pennant in 1931, their left fielder Chick Hafey won the batting title with a .349 average. In addition to a smoking bat, Hafey was one of the league's top defensive outfielders, with a powerful throwing arm. Nevertheless, the following spring the Cardinals dealt Hafey (only twenty-nine years old) to the Reds. The reasons for the stunning deal were twofold: general manager Branch Rickey was irked by Chick's salary demands, and the G.M. knew the team had in their farm system a replacement who was going to be even better than Hafey. His name was Joe Medwick.

Rickey, with his uncanny eye for talent, was absolutely correct about Medwick, who went on to become the National League's top hitter in the 1930s. In addition to his Triple Crown in 1937, Medwick had over 100 RBIs for six consecutive years (leading the league three times in a row), had over 220 hits for three straight years, over 40 doubles seven years running (including a league record 64 in 1936), and was in double figures in triples five straight years.

Born in Carteret, New Jersey, on November 24, 1911, Medwick was known as a "bad-ball hitter."

"There was no way to pitch to him," right-hander Kirby Higbe said. "He hit them off his ankles, around his eyes, inside, outside, it made no difference. And he hit bullets, to left-center, right-center, all over. He was one mean at bat."

Mean on the field and off. His reputation as a surly, hot-tempered, quick-fisted character was in equal renown to his prowess as a hitter. In addition to starting a classic near-riot in the 1934 World Series, Joe once decked Dizzy Dean in the Cardinal dugout after the Great One had the temerity to question Joe's hustle on a ball hit to left field. (Joe was plenty tough, but as Big John Mize said laconically, "He knew who to pick on.")

Medwick played for the Cardinals until June 1940, when he was traded to Brooklyn in a multiplayer deal that also brought the Cardinals a check for $125,000. Soon after, Cardinal pitcher Bob Bowman hit Joe in the head with a fast ball that knocked Medwick cold at home plate. After that, Joe was never again the fearsome hitter he had been.

Medwick later played for the Giants and Braves, returning to St. Louis, where he finished his career as a pinch hitter in 1948. He put in 12 full seasons and in only one of them did he bat under .300. His lifetime average is .324.

Medwick died on March 21, 1975, at the age of sixty-three.

The Yankees added another solid hitter in 1937 with rookie Tommy Henrich. Tommy played in 67 games and batted .320.

Lefty Gomez, who turned in a 21–11 record for the pennant-winning Yankees in 1937.

Yankee outfielder Myril Hoag, a .301 hitter in 1937.

A trio of Giants: *left to right*, pitcher Hal Schumacher, infielder Blondy Ryan, and pitcher Harry Gumbert.

The ace left-handers of the 1937 New York Giant pennant winners: Carl Hubbell (left) and rookie Cliff Melton, who won 20 games.

Giants catcher Harry Danning.

Triple Crown winner Joe Medwick.

Burgess Whitehead, second baseman for the Giants in 1937.

Cardinal left-hander Bob Weiland, a 15–14 pitcher in 1937.

Big Henry Greenberg loosening up at Detroit's Lakeland, Florida, spring training camp.

Lou Fette, one of the Boston Braves' rookie 20-game winners in 1937.

Former Chicago Cub ace Lon Warneke, who was 18–11 for the Cardinals in 1937. A lot of the Cubs felt that trading Warneke (for Rip Collins) cost the team the pennant in 1937.

Charlie Gehringer, 1937 American League batting champion.

Rudy York, a rookie catcher with the Tigers in 1937. He hit 35 home runs and batted .307. Rudy also played some third base that year.

White Sox pitcher Bill Dietrich, who pitched the big leagues' only no-hitter in 1937. It was the highlight of an 8–10 season for him.

Roxie Lawson, who was 18–7 for the Tigers in 1937.

Bob Feller.

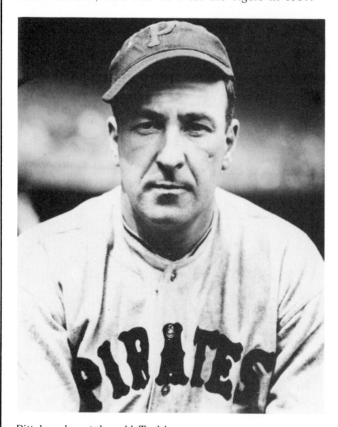

Pittsburgh catcher Al Todd.

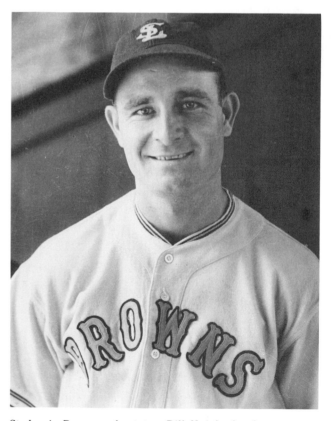

St. Louis Browns shortstop Bill Knickerbocker.

Jim Turner, a rookie 20-game winner for the Braves in 1937.

Washington's Cecil Travis, one of the finest hitting short-stops of all time. In 1937 he batted .344.

Lou Gehrig *(left)* and Dizzy Dean getting together in St. Petersburg during spring training.

Heinie Manush was hitting his line drives for the Dodg-ers this year, enough of them for a .333 batting average.

Pittsburgh second baseman Lee Handley.

Right-hander Jack Wilson, who was 16–10 in 1937.

Pittsburgh right-hander Russ Bauers, who was 13–6 in 1937, his rookie season. Many National League hitters considered him one of the toughest pitchers in the league to hit, but a back injury two years later all but ended his career when he was twenty-five.

Harlond Clift. The St. Louis Browns third baseman was one of the best in the league. In 1937 he hit 29 home runs, drove in 118 runs, and batted .306. Clift never received the recognition due him because, as one writer said, "Playing for the Browns in those years was like playing in the Gobi Desert."

Bobo Newsom was on the move again in 1937, from the Senators to the Red Sox. He was a combined 16–14.

Elbie Fletcher, slick-fielding first baseman of the Boston Braves. He later played for the Pirates.

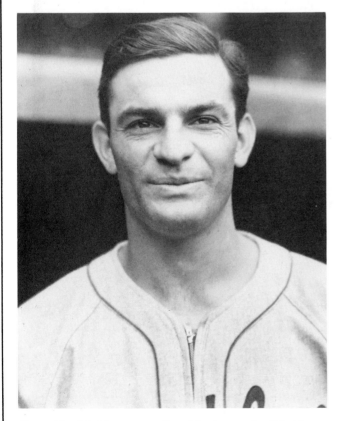

Harry (Cookie) Lavagetto, Brooklyn's popular third baseman.

Hard-boiled Johnny Allen was almost perfect for the Indians in 1937 with a 15–1 record.

Cincinnati's hard-throwing left-hander Lee Grissom *(left)* and manager Charlie Dressen. Lee was 12–17 for his last-place club, but tied for the lead in shutouts with five.

Giants catcher Harry Danning has just tagged the Cubs' Augie Galan out at home. Augie was the front end of an attempted double steal.

Dolf Camilli, hard-hitting first baseman of the Philadel-phia Phillies. In 1937 he hit 27 home runs and batted .339.

Ethan Allen played with six teams during his big-league career, hitting the ball wherever he went. Ethan spent the summer of 1937 in St. Louis with the Browns, batting .316.

Perhaps the most awesome lineup ever—the American League in the 1937 All-Star Game. *Left to right:* Lou Gehrig, Joe Cronin, Bill Dickey, Joe DiMaggio, Charlie Gehringer, Jimmie Foxx, and Hank Greenberg.

In the spring of 1937 the Ohio River went on a rampage and among the sites it flooded was Cincinnati's Crosley Field, the water rising well up into the lower grandstands. That's Reds pitcher Lee Grissom waving his hat in the row boat. Lee and his buddy rowed right over the left-field wall.

Outfielder Mel Almada, who split the 1937 season between the Red Sox and Senators.

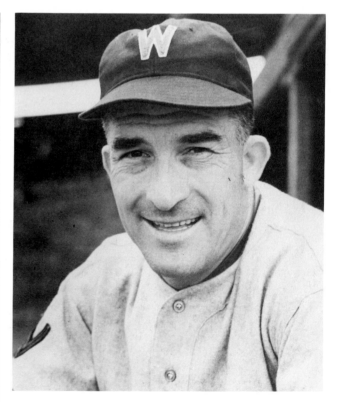

Al Simmons. With Washington in 1937 he dipped to .279.

Dizzy Dean.

Cleveland manager Steve O'Neill *(left)* with his prodigy Bob Feller in April 1937.

Wes Ferrell, who was traded from the Red Sox to the Senators early in the 1937 season. He was a combined 14–19.

Joe DiMaggio unloading his first World Series home run. It came in Game 5 of the 1937 Series against the Giants. The catcher is Harry Danning, the umpire Red Ormsby.

Gabby Hartnett coming home after hitting his memorable "homer in the gloamin'" against the Pirates in late September.

1·9·3·8

It was a year of many stories in baseball, of spectacular individual performances, of poignance and tragedy, of continued Yankee dominance, of one of baseball's most dramatic home runs. But none of the compelling stories of 1938 was bigger than what a little-known Cincinnati left-hander named Johnny Vander Meer achieved on the afternoon of June 11 and the night of June 15.

There was no denying that Vander Meer had talent—he could throw extremely hard—but wildness (which would plague him throughout his career) had been impeding his progress. In 1937, his rookie year, he was just 3–5.

"He'd walk them and he'd strike them out," said Chuck Dressen, Vander Meer's manager in 1937. "He'd drive you nuts, but you had to like him because he had plenty of stuff."

When Bill McKechnie took over the Reds in 1938, he applied his uncanny way with pitchers to Vander Meer, and the young southpaw had this to say about his new manager: "He was one of the greatest individuals I ever met in my life, either on the field or off."

Under McKechnie's skillful tutelage, Vander Meer began finding the strike zone with greater regularity, putting together a fine 15–10 record. But in a pair of back-to-back June starts, Vandy made baseball history; in the realm of short-time individual achievements, no one stands higher in the game's lore than Johnny Vander Meer.

On June 11, the Cincinnati southpaw no-hit the Boston club, 3–0.

"That was the first no-hitter," Vander Meer said years later, "the one that nobody remembers. But without that one there wouldn't have been a second."

The second no-hitter was a festive occasion even before the game began, for it was the game that introduced night baseball to Brooklyn, where Larry MacPhail—who had installed major-league baseball's first lights in Cincinnati in 1935—was now rolling back the night in Ebbets Field. Vander Meer soon made the big occasion an historic one. And in the bottom of the ninth inning his wildness suddenly made it a tense one. One inning away from a second consecutive no-hitter (never done before and not done since), Johnny opened the last of the ninth by retiring the first batter and then walked the bases full. McKechnie came out and settled him down—"I was trying too hard, pressing myself," Vander Meer said, "and he saw that."

Johnny, a native of nearby Prospect Park, New Jersey, did indeed settle down, retiring the next two batters, Ernie Koy and Leo Durocher, and setting what Vander Meer slyly refers to as baseball's "most unbreakable record. After all, to break it," he says, "you'd have to pitch three in a row, right?"

In his next start, Vander Meer started off with three more hitless innings before the string was finally broken, giving him a total of 21 straight innings without yielding a hit.

In the National League pennant race, it looked like a World Series for Pittsburgh, despite a drop-off in batting by their key hitters. After 12 straight years over .300, Paul Waner dropped 74 points to .280, Lloyd Waner fell from .330 to .313, and Al Todd from .307 to .265. Nevertheless, without an ace pitcher, the Pirates held a seven-game lead in early September. At that point they began playing little better than .500 baseball, just at the time the Chicago Cubs were getting hot. (According to

1·9·3·8

their chronological success pattern, this was supposed to be the Cubs' year—they had won in 1929, 1932, and 1935.)

The Cubs had replaced Charlie Grimm as manager with the team's longtime catcher Gabby Hartnett in July, and while most midseason managerial switches are hardly noticeable, this one seemed to make a difference. After playing respectable .556 ball over their first 81 games, the Cubs under Hartnett roared to a 44–27 record and .620 winning percentage the rest of the way.

The Cubs were riding a seven-game winning streak in late September and had moved to within 1½ games of the first-place Pirates, who were coming into Wrigley Field for a three-game series.

The Cubs took the first game, 2–1, behind some gritty pitching by sore-armed Dizzy Dean (7–1 in ten starts that year, and making his first start since August 20). The next game remains one of the most memorable in Cubs history. With the score tied 5–5 in the bottom of the ninth inning, darkness falling, and a tie game an apparent certainty, Hartnett suddenly ripped a pitch from Pirate reliever Mace Brown over the left-field wall for a 6–5 Cub victory and a one-half game lead. The blow stunned the Pirates, who had been expecting a tie game and a doubleheader the following day against a depleted Chicago staff.

"Gabby said he never saw the pitch," Billy Herman said. "It was too damned dark. He just swung where he thought the ball was, and he connected. He really whacked it, too."

It has gone down in National League lore as "The homer in the gloamin'," and it thoroughly demoralized the Pirates, who bowed the next day 10–1. The Cubs went on to win the pennant by two games, keeping intact their curious

three-year pattern (it was broken by the Dodgers in 1941).

Chicago's big pitcher this year was right-hander Bill Lee, a workhorse during the team's sizzling 21–4 September rush. Lee was 22–9 for the year, with nine shutouts and a league-leading 2.66 ERA. Right-hander Clay Bryant was 19–11.

Third baseman Stanley Hack, always a steady hitter, led the club with a .320 batting average. Remarkably, the pennant winners' top RBI man was Augie Galan with 69. The Cubs, in fact, had only one player—Frank Demaree with 115 in 1937—knock in over 100 runs in a season between 1931 and 1942.

The Giants were in the chase for part of the season, but were hurt by Carl Hubbell's sore arm, which trimmed the left-hander to a 13–10 record. "They warned me in 1926 that the screwball would hurt my arm," Hubbell said, adding wryly, "well, in 1938 they were right." Mel Ott's 36 home runs gave him the lead for the fifth time.

The National League's surprise team this year was Cincinnati, finishing fourth, six games behind. It was the Reds' first look into the first division since 1926. Paul Derringer led the staff with a 21–14 record, followed by Vander Meer's 15 wins. The Reds made their key acquisition of Bucky Walters from the Phillies in mid-June, and the converted third baseman was 11–6 for his new team.

Playing his first full season for Cincinnati was first baseman Frank McCormick, who started off in high style with a .327 batting average and a league-leading 209 hits. The Reds also had the batting champion and Most Valuable Player in catcher Ernie Lombardi, who hit .342 and was only the second catcher in big-league history to win a batting title (the

1·9·3·8

Reds' Bubbles Hargrave had done it in 1926).

Joe Medwick slipped a bit from his Triple Crown season, turning in a .322 average but leading in RBIs for the third straight year with 122, tying a record held by Ty Cobb, Babe Ruth, Honus Wagner, and Rogers Hornsby, which was as elegant as it got in baseball. Joe's Cardinal teammate Johnny Mize was second in the batting race to Lombardi with a .337 average.

With mutterings of regret from the hitters and sighs of relief from the pitchers, on July 4, the Philadelphia Phillies, after 51 years, vacated archaic Baker Bowl and its neighborly fences and moved in to share Shibe Park with the Athletics.

Behind the strong pitching of Vander Meer, Lee, and Brown, the National League beat the American in the All-Star Game by a score of 4–1.

There was some magisterial power hitting in the American League in 1938, turned in by Boston's Jimmie Foxx and Detroit's Hank Greenberg. Jimmie, the league's MVP for the third time, hit 50 home runs, drove in 175 runs (fourth highest total in major-league history), and batted .349 to win the batting crown. Greenberg belted 58 homers and drove in 146 runs, while batting .315.

"Jimmie hit 50 homers and wasn't close to leading," Greenberg said, "and I drove in 146 runs and wasn't close to leading. That was a hell of a year."

Despite having two men with 50 home runs, it still was not a big home-run year in the league for individuals—the Browns' Harlond Clift was third with 34—but a new American League record was set with 864 homers.

The Yankees didn't have anyone leading the league in any significant offensive categories;

nevertheless, the New Yorkers took their third straight pennant, winning by 9½ games over the Red Sox. Joe McCarthy's team took over the lead from a pitching-rich Cleveland outfit in mid-July and, in the parlance of baseball, "ran away and hid."

The Yankee attack was deadly and methodic. Although outhit by the Red Sox by a considerable margin—.299 to .274—and by four other teams as well, the New Yorkers led in runs scored with 966. The Red Sox had six .300 hitters in their regular lineup, the Yankees but three; the Yankee hitting, however, was harder and more equitably distributed. The Red Sox had Foxx with his 50 homers, but only one other Boston player—Joe Cronin with 17—reached double figures in home runs. The Yankees had five men with 20 or more home runs, topped by DiMaggio's 32.

For the Yankees of those years, the 1938 team was fairly typical—stars departing, stars arriving. With the departure of their veteran second baseman Tony Lazzeri, the team brought up from their fertile farm system to replace him Joe Gordon, who broke in with 25 homers and 97 RBIs. Another addition was outfielder Tommy Henrich, who hit 22 homers and had 91 RBIs. The new men joined the established Yankee stars that already included DiMaggio, Bill Dickey, George Selkirk, Red Rolfe, and Lou Gehrig.

No one knew it then, but 1938 was the twilight year for Lou Gehrig. His record indicates that the insidious and fatal illness that was to take his life three years later was already dropping its noose around him. Gehrig finished the season playing in his 2,122nd consecutive game, going into the winter with his lowest batting average (.295) since 1925, lowest home-run total (29) since 1928, and lowest

1·9·3·8

RBI total (114) since 1926. The muscle deterioration caused by the amyotrophic lateral sclerosis from which he was suffering accelerated so quickly that he was, after the 1938 World Series, for all intents and purposes finished as a baseball player.

To go along with his sturdy lineup, McCarthy also had four strong starters: Red Ruffing (21–7), Lefty Gomez (18–12), Monte Pearson (16–7), and Spud Chandler (14–5).

"Don't forget those pitchers," Joe McCarthy once admonished a writer. "When people talk about the Yankees, all you hear is Ruth and Gehrig and DiMaggio and Dickey and all those other great hitters. But the reason we won so many pennants was because we had the best pitching. Don't forget it."

Along with Foxx, the Red Sox got .300 seasons from Cronin, third baseman Pinky Higgins, and outfielders Joe Vosmik, Ben Chapman, and Doc Cramer. Higgins established a new major-league record when he whacked out 12 consecutive hits over the course of two doubleheaders on June 19 and 21. The lowest average among Red Sox regulars belonged to their rookie second baseman Bobby Doerr, who began his career as the greatest second baseman in the club's history with a .289 average.

Boston's thirty-eight-year-old Lefty Grove, his once mighty fast ball now part of baseball history, used guile and know-how and slow curves and posted a 14–4 record and won his eighth ERA title (3.07).

When Cleveland right-hander Johnny Allen suffered an arm injury in the middle of the season, it dampened whatever chances the Indians had of bringing September excitement to the shores of Lake Erie. Allen finished up with a 14–8 record, while Mel Harder was 17–10 and

Bob Feller 17–11. The nineteen-year-old Feller, in his first full season, led in strikeouts with 240, which was the highest in the league since young Bobby's predecessor among right-handed supermen pitchers, Walter Johnson, fanned 243 in 1913. Feller also walked 208 batters (a major-league record), which meant that standing up there against his 100-mph fast ball could be a chancy assignment.

Standing up at home plate against Feller on the final day of the season was Detroit's Hank Greenberg, with 58 home runs in hand and a chance to tie or maybe even break Ruth's record. The Tigers and Indians had a doubleheader scheduled and Feller was on the mound in the opener. Newsreel cameras were at the park, in position to record baseball history, in the event Big Henry made it. Well, the cameras got their history, but it wasn't Greenberg who made it; it was on this day that Blazing Bob fanned 18 batters to set a new one-game strikeout record. The best Greenberg could do was a double in four at bats; in the second game he had three singles—minnows for a man in search of bigger game—and completed his season with those 58 home runs, tying him with Foxx for the most ever dispatched by a right-handed batter.

The American League batted .281, a figure it has not since topped. Nearly thirty regulars were over .300, though with Foxx's .349 leading, there were no truly lush averages. Cleveland's Jeff Heath, in his first full year, was second to Foxx with a .343 mark, while his teammates Hal Trosky (.334) and Earl Averill (.330) helped sustain a strong attack.

With a team average of .293, fifth-place Washington had five .300 stickers in the regular lineup, including one of the sharpest hitting double-play combinations of all time—

1·9·3·8

shortstop Cecil Travis (.335) and second baseman Buddy Myer (.336).

In addition to Ruffing, Bobo Newsom was also a 20-game winner, going 20–16 for the seventh-place Browns, pitching 330 innings. ("He had a rubber arm and a head to match," one player said of the gregarious, happy-go-lucky Bobo.) One of the better young pitchers in the league was Chicago White Sox right-hander Monty Stratton, a 15-game winner for the second year in a row. That fall, however, the twenty-six-year-old pitcher was accidentally shot in the leg in a hunting mishap, costing him his leg and his career. (Stratton's career, accident, and game attempt at a comeback were the subject of a 1949 film, *The Stratton Story*, featuring James Stewart.)

The World Series was a routine Yankee sweep of the Cubs, with the only drama supplied by Dizzy Dean in Game 2. Where once there had been an elastic arm and hopping fast ball, now there was an aching arm and a maze of carefully controlled slow curves. Dean hoodwinked the Yankee bomb squad for seven innings, taking a 3–2 lead into the top of the eighth, but then the light-hitting Frank Crosetti hit a two-run homer and in the top of the ninth DiMaggio drew down the curtain on Dizzy Dean's final moment on center stage with another two-run homer.

The Yankees were now the first team to win three straight world championships.

Gehrig playing in his 2,000th consecutive game in June 1938.

Hank Greenberg.

Hank Greenberg

"No power hitter ever looked better standing up at the plate," said Paul Richards about Hank Greenberg. "He stood almost straight up, with that bat cocked high behind his right ear, and he was a picture of confidence. I used to think of two things when I saw Hank standing at home plate: he knows he can hit, and he enjoys it."

The big boy began drawing attention playing for the James Monroe High School team in the Bronx, hitting long balls that reminded some observers of the shots launched a few years before by another New York high schooler, Lou Gehrig. Gehrig, ironically, was one of Greenberg's early problems.

"I used to go to Yankee Stadium," Greenberg said, "and I'd look at Gehrig, at that powerful physique, and I'd say to myself that the Yankees had a first baseman that was going to last a long time."

So Greenberg tried out with the neighborhood's other big-league team, the Giants. Despite always being on the lookout for a Jewish player who might be a good gate attraction, the Giants somehow overlooked young Henry Greenberg, who eventually signed with the Tigers.

Greenberg came to the big leagues with Detroit in 1933 and a year later was a star, launching a career that would see him voted the American League's Most Valuable Player in 1935 and 1940.

Big Henry's major-league career included just nine full seasons, thanks to one year out with a broken wrist (1936) and four-and-a-half years in military service. Nevertheless, there was time enough for him to put together some very impressive power statistics, in home runs, runs batted in, and slugging percentage. His 58 home runs in 1938 tie him with Jimmie Foxx for most ever by a right-handed hitter, his 183 runs batted in in 1937 are one under Gehrig's American League record, and his .605 lifetime slugging percentage places him fifth on the all-time list.

Four times the Detroit slugger led in home runs and four times in RBIs, while compiling a lifetime average of .313. His greatest single moment on a baseball diamond came in the last game of the 1945 season. After leaving the service in July, Greenberg rejoined the Tigers and helped them battle the Washington Senators in a close pennant race that went down to the final day. Needing a victory to clinch, the Tigers won it on a ninth-inning grand-slam home run by Big Henry.

After leading the American League in home runs and runs batted in, in 1946, Greenberg was waived to the Pittsburgh Pirates, for whom he played for one year and then retired.

Greenberg died on September 4, 1986, at the age of seventy-five.

Bill Lee, who was 22–9 for the pennant-winning Chicago Cubs in 1938.

Cubs right-hander Clay Bryant, a 19–11 pitcher for the team in 1938.

Cubs second baseman Billy Herman.

Lou Gehrig.

Mace Brown, the Pittsburgh reliever who threw the fatal pitch to Hartnett.

Johnny Vander Meer.

Johnny Vander Meer at work on his second consecutive no-hitter at Ebbets Field on June 15, 1938.

Johnny Vander Meer being escorted off the field by a pair of jacketed teammates moments after completing his second straight no-hitter.

Yankee rookie second baseman Joe Gordon, one of five Yankees to have over 20 home runs in 1938.

Cleveland's young slugger Jeff Heath. He batted .343 in 1938 and led the league in triples with 18.

Joe DiMaggio.

It looks like DiMaggio has just lofted a deep one. Note
that photographers were allowed on the field in those
days and how dangerously close they sometimes
approached.

Bob Feller.

Johnny Murphy, the Yankees' ace reliever in the 1930s.

Ernie Lombardi. The Cincinnati catcher was the National League batting champion in 1938.

Detroit's slugging catcher Rudy York. He had 33 homers in 1938.

Cleveland shortstop Lyn Lary. He played for seven big-league clubs in the 1930s.

Cleveland's Rollie Hemsley, one of the outstanding defensive catchers of his time.

Johnny Mize. The Cardinal first baseman batted .337 in 1938 and led the league in triples with 16.

Cincinnati first baseman Frank McCormick getting on top of things in spring training. Frank led the National League with 209 hits in his rookie year.

Pinky Higgins has just connected for his record-making 12th consecutive hit on June 21. The Red Sox third baseman batted .303 in 1938.

The St. Louis Cardinal outfield in 1938: *left to right,* rookie Enos Slaughter, Terry Moore, and Joe Medwick.

Cleveland catcher Frankie Pytlak, who was a .308 hitter in 1938.

Dixie Walker, who batted .308 for the Tigers in 1938.

Lefty Grove, the American League's ERA leader in 1938.

Cardinal catcher Mickey Owen.

Cardinal infielder Jimmy Brown, a .301 hitter in 1938.

Chicago Cubs rookie Kirby Higbe, who later became an ace right-hander with the Phillies and Dodgers.

Johnny Rizzo, Pittsburgh's rookie outfielder, who batted .301 and drove in 111 runs.

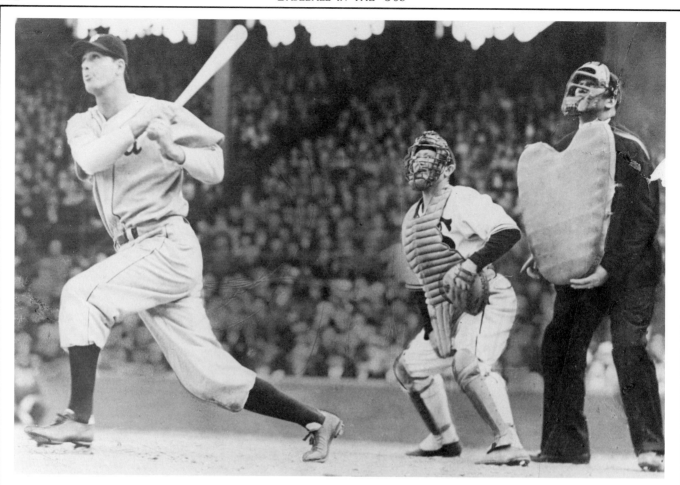

Hank Greenberg hit 58 home runs in 1938, and this is number 1. It came on opening day against the White Sox at Comiskey Park. The catcher is Tony Rensa, the umpire Cal Hubbard.

The Pirates' Gus Suhr is caught in what sandlotters used to call a "pickle." Giants shortstop Dick Bartell is at the left and the man receiving the ball is first baseman Johnny McCarthy. The umpire is Bill Stewart. The action occurred at the Polo Grounds.

A quintet of Detroit outfielders: *left to right,* Pete Fox, Dixie Walker, Roy Cullenbine, Jo-Jo White, and Chet Laabs.

Tony Lazzeri. The former Yankee second baseman turned up with the Cubs in 1938 and found himself on another pennant winner.

George McQuinn. The Browns first baseman batted .324 in his first full season.

Jimmie Foxx is just crossing home plate after a home run while an enthusiastic fan has come running out to celebrate the occasion. Number 4 is Joe Cronin.

Jimmie Foxx. Jimmie hit 50 homers in 1938 and wasn't even close to leading the league. His 175 RBIs and .349 batting average, however, were tops in the league.

Monty Stratton.

The 'White Sox' Mike Kreevich.

Phillies right-hander Bucky Walters, who was traded to the Reds in June. Bucky was 11–6 for the Reds, 15–14 overall.

Washington third baseman Buddy Lewis, a .296 hitter in 1938.

Brooklyn general manager Larry MacPhail watching a game in progress at Ebbets Field in 1938.

Dodgers outfielder Ernie Koy, a .299 hitter in 1938.

The Cubs' Stan Hack is safe at third while Cookie Lavagetto waits for the throw.

Philadelphia Athletics catcher Frank Hayes. He later caught for four other American League teams.

George Caster, who was 16–20 for the last-place Athletics in 1938, the biggest win total of his 12-year career.

Pittsburgh's Arky Vaughan, a .322 hitter in 1938.

Dario Lodigiani, second baseman for the Athletics.

Cincinnati third baseman Lew Riggs.

The rival managers giving each other five during the 1938 World Series. That's the Cubs' Gabby Hartnett *(left)* and the Yankees' Joe McCarthy. When McCarthy had managed the Cubs years earlier, Gabby was his catcher.

Don Padgett had just 233 at bats for the Cardinals in 1939, but he made superb use of them, batting .399.

1·9·3·9

The Cincinnati Reds won their first pennant in 20 years and they did it on the strength of the tremendous pitching of Bucky Walters and Paul Derringer. Walters, the one-time infielder who had resisted the transition to the mound, earned the Most Valuable Player Award with a 27–11 season and league-leading figures in earned-run average (2.29), strikeouts (137), and complete games (31). And just for good measure, the former third baseman batted .325. Derringer was equally impressive, with a 25–7 record and .781 winning percentage, best in the league. The two right-handers combined for 52 of Cincinnati's 97 wins, which gave Bill McKechnie's club—in eighth place just two years before—a 4½-game bulge over the second-place Cardinals at the end of the season.

Using a 12-game winning streak as a springboard, the Reds took over first place for keeps in May and had a smooth ride to the finish line, with only a late September threat from the Cardinals causing some concern.

"The Cardinals gave us a few gray hairs at the end," Reds first baseman Frank McCormick said, "but we had just enough hitting, good defense, and most of all we had Paul and Bucky. They never gave in."

The Cincinnati hitting was indeed "just enough" and not more. They were outhit by the Cardinals, .294 to .278, as well as outscored. McCormick led the Reds with a .332 batting average and again topped the league in hits with 209, as well as in RBIs with 128. Outfielder Ival Goodman backed up McCormick with a .323 mark. The Reds' other big hitter was catcher Ernie Lombardi at .287. The big, slow-footed Lombardi was by general agreement the league's hardest hitter. Because of his almost total lack of running speed, the left side of the infield often played him back on the edge of the outfield grass where, McCormick said, "it was safer. Ernie hit the ball murderously hard. Playing at normal depth, the third baseman was in mortal danger."

Filling out the rest of McKechnie's team were Lonny Frey at second, Billy Myers at short, Bill Werber at third, and Harry Craft and the veteran Wally Berger in the outfield. Right-handers Junior Thompson and Whitey Moore backed up Walters and Derringer with 13 wins apiece. The miracle man of 1938, Johnny Vander Meer, was slowed by arm problems to a 5–9 record.

A realignment was taking place in the National League as the Cubs and Giants, who between them had taken the previous four pennants, now finished fourth and fifth, respectively. The coming teams were the Cardinals and Dodgers, who in 1941 and 1942 would put on two of the more grueling pennant races in National League history.

In 1939, the Cards jumped from sixth place the year before to second. First baseman Johnny Mize was the batting champ with a .349 average and the home-run leader with 28, one more than the Giants' Ott and two better than Brooklyn first baseman Dolf Camilli. Joe Medwick batted .332 and young outfielder Enos Slaughter, in his second year, hit .320. In Terry Moore, the Cards had the man considered the top defensive center fielder in the league (who was also a .295 hitter). The team's backup catcher Don Padgett, who came to bat 233 times, turned in a sky-high .399 batting average, which was definitely out of character— Don was a .288 lifetime hitter. Right-hander

1·9·3·9

Curt Davis (22–16) was the big winner for the Cardinals.

Rising from a half dozen years of doldrums, the Brooklyn Dodgers, under new manager Leo Durocher, finished third. The Dodgers got a surprise 20–13 season from right-hander Luke Hamlin and some power hitting from Camilli (26 homers, 104 RBIs).

The fading New York Giants had a forgettable season, except for one particularly thunderous inning on June 6. On their way to a 17–3 manhandling of the Reds, the Giants exploded with a record five home runs in the fourth inning, struck by Harry Danning, Frank Demaree, Burgess Whitehead, pitcher Manny Salvo, and Jo-Jo Moore. For Whitehead it was one of two home runs he hit all season and for Salvo the only one.

The American League won the All-Star Game, 3–1, thanks in large part to some strong relief pitching by Feller.

The 1939 New York Yankees won 106 games and became the second team in baseball history to win four consecutive pennants (McGraw's 1921–24 Giants had done it previously). Remarkably, this 106-game-winning team had just one big winner on its pitching staff—Red Ruffing at 21–7—who was followed by a half dozen modest but highly efficient pitchers: Atley Donald (13–3), Lefty Gomez (12–8), Bump Hadley (12–6), Monte Pearson (12–5), Steve Sundra (11–1), and Oral Hildebrand (10–4).

"I had a lot of good pitchers," Joe McCarthy said, "and I used them all."

The New Yorkers pounded American League pitching for a .287 average, led by MVP Joe DiMaggio's .381, the league's best and The Yankee Clipper's career high. A late-season slump cost DiMaggio a shot at batting .400.

As was their habit in those years, the Yankees introduced into their lineup another shimmering new talent in outfielder Charlie Keller, a muscular twenty-two-year-old youngster who batted .334. Third baseman Red Rolfe was at .329 this year, rapping out a league-leading 213 hits, while George Selkirk (.306) and Bill Dickey (.302) gave the club five .300 hitters among the regulars. DiMaggio, Selkirk, Dickey, and Joe Gordon each drove in over 100 runs. From August 9–25 Rolfe set a major-league record by scoring at least 1 run (30 altogether) in 18 straight games.

Missing from this litany of Yankee slugging splendor was the name of Lou Gehrig. ("Only the Yankees," one writer said, "could lose Lou Gehrig and still win the pennant with ease.") After playing eight games, during which he was able to manage just four singles and one RBI in 28 at bats, Gehrig took himself out of the lineup in Detroit on May 2.

The erstwhile Iron Man's physical condition had deteriorated shockingly over the winter. When spring training began it was apparent to everyone that there was something seriously wrong with the veteran first baseman. His coordination and reflexes were gone, his movements on the field slow, awkward, clumsy. The amiable clubhouse raillery about "getting old" soon ceased, followed by discreet silence and averted glances. The Yankee players knew that their longtime star was suffering; that he was a dying man was still too farfetched to consider.

McCarthy watched and waited. The skipper had two things to take into account: the good of the team and the pride of "my favorite player," who was virtually a surrogate son. There was also that incredible 14-year-old streak,

1·9·3·9

which by May 2 had extended to 2,130 games.

"I knew there was something wrong with Lou," McCarthy said, "but I didn't know what it was. His reflexes were shot. I was afraid of his getting hit with a pitched ball. He wouldn't have been able to get out of the way, that's how bad it was. That was my chief concern, to get him out of there before he got hurt."

Gehrig and McCarthy talked in the manager's hotel room on the night of May 1.

"He asked me how much longer he should stay in," McCarthy said. "I told him I thought it was best if he got out right now. He agreed with me. 'I'm not doing the ball club any good,' he said."

Lou was replaced at first base by Babe Dahlgren, who hit 15 home runs, drove in 89 runs, and batted .235. (Baseball's greatest team had to wait 45 years, until 1984 and the arrival of Don Mattingly, before it had another genuine star at first base.)

Gehrig went to the Mayo Clinic in Rochester, Minnesota, where one look at him told the doctors that the Iron Man was doomed.

"The vacant look in his eyes and the shuffling gait told us all we had to know," one doctor said.

July 4 was declared "Lou Gehrig Appeciation Day" and between games of a doubleheader at Yankee Stadium Gehrig made a simple, highly emotional farewell speech in which he described himself "as the luckiest man on the face of the earth." Less than two years later he was dead.

In late April, the paths of Gehrig and his immediate successor as baseball's greatest left-handed power hitter briefly crossed. The Boston Red Sox had in their lineup a rookie twenty-year-old with a swing that was devastating and poetically pure. Tall, lanky, handsome,

sometimes maddeningly temperamental, Ted Williams soon became baseball's "most charismatic at bat since Ruth." Beginning a career dedicated to becoming "the greatest hitter that ever lived," Williams batted .327, hit 31 home runs, and led the league with a rookie record 145 runs batted in. His first hit came at Yankee Stadium on April 20, a long two-bagger, and the man he passed as he went churning around first base was the nearly immobilized Lou Gehrig.

Finishing second, 17 games out, the Red Sox batted .291, boasting four other .300 hitters in the lineup besides Williams. Jimmie Foxx, having his last herculean season, batted .360 and led the league with 35 home runs. Bobby Doerr hit .318; Doc Cramer, .311; and Joe Cronin, .308. But, as ever, the Red Sox were short on quality pitching. Their top winner was the thirty-nine-year-old Lefty Grove, who was 15–4 with the league's best ERA, 2.54, the ninth time he had won this coveted distinction, by far the major-league record.

Cleveland finished third, 20½ games behind, despite the burst to superstardom by Bob Feller. Now all of twenty years old, "the Cleveland marvel" was 24–9 with a league-leading 246 strikeouts. The Indians received some productive hitting from first baseman Hal Trosky (.335) and sophomore third baseman Ken Keltner (.325). Two years later Keltner would make two dazzling stops of hard-hit DiMaggio ground balls that would contribute to the snapping of Joe's 56-game hitting streak, casting Keltner forever into the wake of the mighty DiMaggio craft.

Detroit's Hank Greenberg dropped from 58 home runs to 33, two behind Foxx, while Washington outfielder George Case stole 51 bases to lead for the first of five consecutive

Lou Gehrig (left) and Joe McCarthy. Time had all but run out on the Iron Man.

Charlie Keller. A rookie in 1939, Keller broke in with a .334 batting average and had a sensational World Series against the Reds.

Cincinnati first baseman Frank McCormick. He batted .332 in 1939 and led the league with 209 hits and 128 RBIs.

seasons. Case's teammate, knuckleballer Dutch Leonard, was 20–8 for the sixth-place Senators.

Early in May, the Tigers acquired Bobo Newsom from the Browns in a ten-player transaction and the much-traveled Bobo won 17 games for Detroit, which, added to the three he had taken with the Browns, made him a 20-game winner for the second year in a row.

On May 16, the Philadelphia Athletics hosted the Indians under Shibe Park's newly installed lights, marking the first night game in American League history.

The Yankees made it two sweeps and four world championships in a row when they rubbed out the Reds in four straight. Ruffing, Pearson, and Hadley did some excellent pitching, while the hitting star was the rookie Keller. Charlie dismantled the Reds' fine pitching almost single-handedly with a .438 average, hitting three home runs and driving in six runs. (The cry across the baseball landscape by now was "Break up the Yankees," while in Cincinnati it was more modest: "Yankees, hell. Just break up Keller.")

The World Series was marked by "the Lombardi snooze" at home plate in the tenth inning of the final game, during which the Yankees scored three runs. With Crosetti on third and Keller on first, DiMaggio ripped a single to right, scoring Crosetti. When the ball was fumbled in the outfield, Keller also came around and on a play at the plate barreled into Lombardi, knocking the ball loose and momentarily stunning the big catcher. Seeing the dazed Lombardi lying on the ground, the ball nearby, the ever-alert DiMaggio also came in to score. Thus the story of Lombardi's "snooze"—a story patently unfair to Ernie.

"It was a dull Series," Bucky Walters said, "and they had nothing else to write about, so they picked on poor old Ernie. It was the big story and it was no story."

As the 1939 season was winding down, a little-noted event took place at Ebbets Field on August 26. On this afternoon NBC-TV brought its cameras to the park to televise a big-league game for the first time, a doubleheader between the Dodgers and Reds. The radius of coverage was about 50 miles, the television sets then in use a mere handful. It was the first trickle of an oncoming Mississippi.

Bob Feller.

Bob Feller

Bob Feller has been described as "baseball's only prodigy," and the Iowa farmboy was indeed that, and more. Not only was he a teenager striking out big-league batters in record numbers, but he was doing it at a time when batters struck out with far less frequency than they did in later years.

Feller wasn't just fast; he was fast enough to become a legend-in-the-making from the first time he pitched from a big-league mound.

Feller was born in Van Meter, Iowa, on November 3, 1918, son of a corn and hog farmer whose dream it was to see his boy pitch in the big leagues. It is now part of the folklore of baseball how William Feller coached the strapping youngster, caught the ever accelerating fast ball in the back yard and then in the winter in the barn, and even designed and built a small ball park on the family's meadowland.

Also part of the Feller story is how Cleveland scout Cy Slapnicka came to Iowa at the behest of some local umpires, saw the boy pitch, signed him for a bonus of one dollar and returned to Cleveland to announce he had discovered "the greatest pitcher that ever lived."

Robert William Andrew Feller was as singular an individualist as ever played America's game, a man who lived by his own admirable credo. He never resented not receiving the huge bonus that would have been his had he waited another year or two before signing.

"I figured if I was worth big money, I'd make it later," he said, "after I'd proved I was worth it. And if I wasn't worth it, then I had no business having it."

In time he became, of course, one of the highest-paid players of his time, the first to have attendance clauses written into his contracts.

Throwing America's most famous fast ball, which was complemented by a hard-breaking curve that one batter called "pure evil," Feller put together three blazing seasons just before the war—24–9, 27–11, and 25–13. He joined the Navy several days after Pearl Harbor and did not return until the middle of the 1945 season.

'Rapid Robert" was a 26-game winner in 1946, a 20-game winner in 1947, and in 1951 his 22 victories put him in pitching's select circle for the sixth and final time.

As in the case of Ted Williams, the years Feller lost to military service remain tantalizing gaps in his record. How many more games would he have won? How many more men would he have struck out? How many more no-hitters? But even without the missing years, there is more than enough of everything: 266 victories (against 162 defeats), 6 times leading in victories, 7 times in strikeouts, 3 no-hitters, 12 one-hitters. And that imperishable legend.

Oral Hildebrand, who was 10–4 for the pennant-winning
Yankees in 1939.

Joe DiMaggio.

Atley Donald, another high-percentage winner for the
1939 Yankees with a 13–3 record.

Steve Sundra, who was 11–1 for McCarthy's Yankees in
1939.

Paul Derringer, 25–7 for the Reds in 1939.

A bit of action from the 1939 All-Star Game, played at Yankee Stadium that year. Detroit's Hank Greenberg (Number 5) has just retired the Reds' Frank McCormick at first base.

Outfielder Ival Goodman, who batted .323 for the pennant-winning 1939 Reds.

Cincinnati center fielder Harry Craft, one of the finest defensive outfielders of his time.

Cincinnati Reds manager Bill McKechnie.

Ernie Lombardi.

Bucky Walters, who was 27–11 for the Reds in 1939.

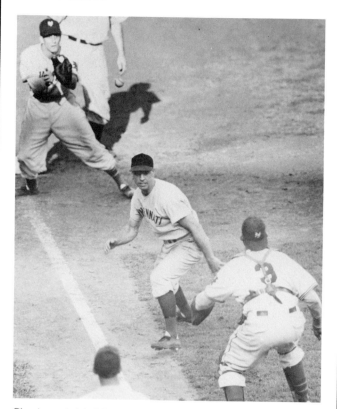

Cincinnati third baseman Billy Werber has been caught in a rundown. Narrowing the gap on him are New York Giants catcher Harry Danning (Number 3) and pitcher Bill Lohrman, who is covering the bag.

Bobby Doerr, the talented young second baseman of the Boston Red Sox. A second-year man in 1939, Bobby batted .318.

Lefty Grove. At the age of thirty-nine, he was 15–4 for the Red Sox and won his ninth and last ERA title. No other pitcher has led in ERA more than five times.

An unknown rookie at the time, this youngster tore apart the Dodgers' spring training camp in 1939. Two years later Pete Reiser was a twenty-two-year-old batting champion.

Cincinnati second baseman Lonny Frey.

Red Sox left-hander Fritz Ostermueller, one of the team's more successful pitchers in the 1930s.

The new man in the American League: Boston's Ted Williams.

Brooklyn's Van Mungo. By 1939 some of the hurry was gone from his fast ball.

Left to right: Lefty Gomez, Lou Gehrig, and Jimmie Foxx. Lou had by now played his final game.

Brooklyn's Italian contingent in spring training, 1939. *Left to right:* Tony Lazzeri, Dolf Camilli, and Cookie Lavagetto. Be assured that Dolf's facial decoration was gone by opening day.

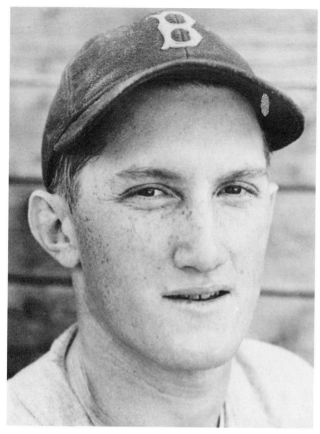

The Red Sox' hard-hitting rookie third baseman Jim Tabor. In 1939, his first full season, Jim knocked in 95 runs.

Dodger right-hander Luke Hamlin, a surprise 20-game winner in 1939.

Dolf Camilli in levitation.

Cardinals manager Ray Blades *(left)* and his star slugger Joe Medwick at the Cardinals' St. Petersburg camp in the spring of 1939. Joe had just ended a month-long holdout.

Curt Davis. He was 22–16 for the Cardinals in 1939.

Big John Mize at bat. Notice how these sluggers are almost always looking up after they connect.

Vince DiMaggio doesn't seem at all upset after being sent back to the minors by the Boston Braves in February 1939. Vince was back in the bigs a year later with Cincinnati.

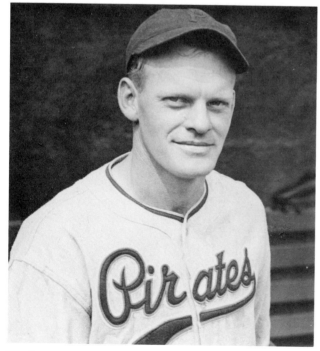

Pittsburgh right-hander Rip Sewell. In the early 1940s he became famous for throwing the "blooper" pitch.

Cleveland's Al Milnar, who won 14 games for the Indians in 1939.

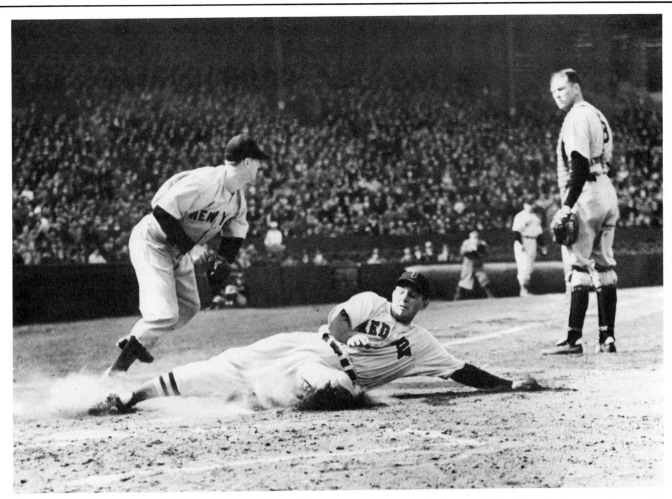

The Red Sox' Lou Finney is out at home in this play at Yankee Stadium. Yankee pitcher Monte Pearson has made the putout, while catcher Bill Dickey looks on.

Barney McCosky, Detroit's rookie outfielder, who broke in with a .311 batting average.

Taft Wright. The sharp-hitting outfielder batted .309 for Washington in 1939, then was traded to the White Sox.

Brooklyn Dodger second baseman Pete Coscarart.

Morrie Arnovich. The Phillies outfielder had his best year in 1939, batting .324.

Babe Dahlgren, Gehrig's replacement at first base. Babe hit only .235 in 1939 but did drive in 89 runs.

Cleveland's fine young third baseman Ken Keltner, who batted .325 in 1939.

Phillies pitcher Hugh Mulcahy, a talented right-hander who was always saddled with losing teams.

Whitey Moore, the third starter behind Walters and Derringer on the 1939 Reds. Whitey was 13–12.

A couple of long-ball hitters: Rudy York (left) and Bob Johnson. Johnson drove in over 100 runs for the Athletics for seven consecutive years, from 1935 through 1941. His .338 batting average in 1939 was the highest of his career.

Cincinnati right-hander Gene Thompson, a 13–5 pitcher for the pennant winners in 1939. He pitched primarily in relief.

Billy Myers, the shortstop for Cincinnati's pennant winners in 1939.

Washington's Dutch Leonard, who featured a knuckle ball. He was 20–8 in 1939.

Chicago White Sox left-hander Edgar Smith.

Athletics outfielder Sam Chapman.

Washington coach Clyde Milan *(center)* is flanked by a pair of budding stars: first baseman Mickey Vernon *(left)* and outfielder George Case. Case led the league with 51 stolen bases in 1939. Vernon later won two American League batting titles.

Dick Siebert, Athletics first baseman who batted .294 in 1939.

The ace of the White Sox staff in 1939 was right-hander Johnny Rigney, who had a 15–8 record.

Red Rolfe scoring a Yankee run in the 1939 World Series. Joe DiMaggio (bats in hand) and the Yankee bat boy are watching. The catcher is Ernie Lombardi.

The famous Lombardi "snooze" in the 10th inning of the fourth and final game of the 1939 World Series. Joe DiMaggio has just slid across the plate as a dazed Lombardi lies on the ground. Reds pitcher Bucky Walters is at the right. The umpire is Babe Pinelli.

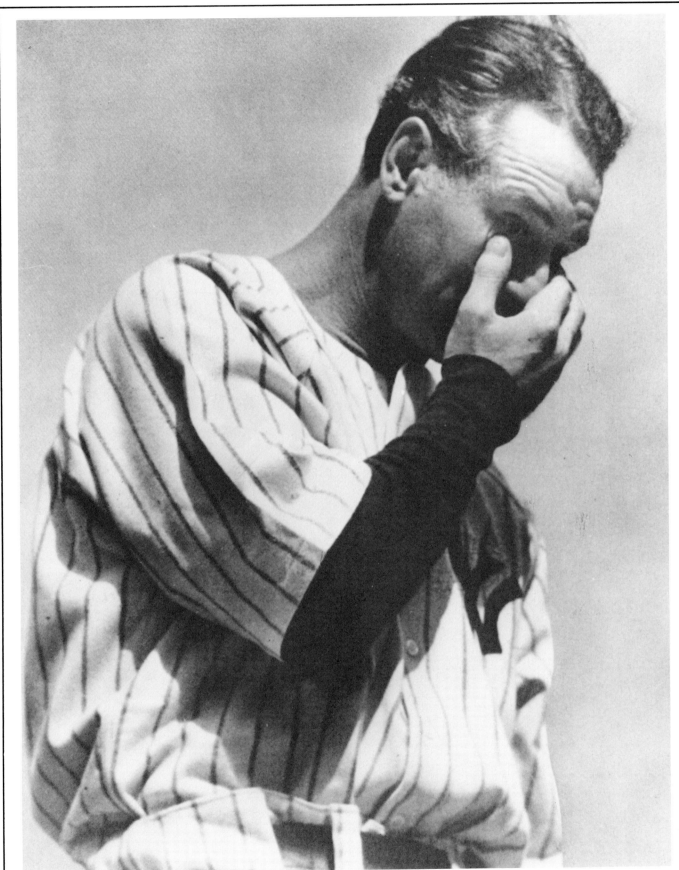

It's "Lou Gehrig Appreciation Day" at Yankee Stadium on July 4, 1939, and the guest of honor is trying to fight back the tears.

Index